A Daily Dose of Godly Encouragement: Medicine for Tough Days

Book I: Winter

Larry E Davies

Table of Contents

January	**1**
1 – The Little Church that Could!	2
2 – Resolutions & John the Baptist	4
3 – Aprons: A Symbol of Service	6
4 – Anger & Grace	8
5 – God and the Church	10
6 – Shoveling Snow	12
7 – Prayer: Looking Within	14
8 – Winter Shelter	16
9 – "Stairway to Heaven"	18
10 – Cat-Kicking	20
11 – Cat-Kicking – Answers	23
12 – $10 Challenge	25
13 – $10 Challenge Stories	27
14 – More $10 Challenge Stories	29
15 – A Tornado and Two Churches	31
16 – 1 Tornado, 2 Churches = One New Church Building	34
17 – Brokenness to Reconciliation	36
18 – Pandemic Memories	38
19 – Monopoly	41
20 – Instrument of Peace	43
21 – Ten Old Testament Action Words	45
22 – Three Emails	47
23 – "Stop! Hey, What's that Sound?"	49

24 – Stumbling   51
25 – Stumbling & Job   54
26 – Comfort   56
27 – Three Funerals   58
28 – Prayer for a Dead Church   60
29 – "Hang in There?"   62
30 – God's Relief for Anxiety   64
31 – Are You the Messiah?   66

February   **68**
1 – An Audacious Miracle   69
2 – An Audacious Miracle – Conclusion   71
3 – A Servant   73
4 – Persistent Prayer   75
5 – Riding a Dead Horse   77
6 – Storms & John Wesley   79
7 – John Wesley & Faith   81
8 – A Bear & Running Shoes   83
9 – $7.43   85
10 – $7.43 Lives On   87
11 – "The Impossible Dream"   89
12 – "The Impossible Dream" Lives On   91
13 – Humble Pie   93
14 – Love and Weddings   95
15 – "Free, Free, Free"   97
16 – Awareness   99
17 – "It's Your Church. It's God's Church"   101
18 – The Church: Judgment   103

19 – The Church: Encouragement — 105
20 – Sam — 107
21 – God & Money — 110
22 – Stuck in the Mud — 112
23 – Tap, Tap, Tap: Worship — 114
24 – Nine Miracles — 117
25 – Something — 120
26 – Empty Chairs — 123
27 – Disaster Response — 125
28 – "We Are the Church" — 127

March — **129**
1 – The Thermostat War — 130
2 – Ron — 132
3 – "No Pain? No Gain!" — 134
4 – Snakes and Shepherds — 136
5 – Lent — 138
6 – The Church: Supporting Each Other — 140
7 – Pick Up Your Cross and Fly — 142
8 – "I Just Wanted Mulch!" — 145
9 – Church Stories — 148
10 – Evangelism? — 151
11 – "One Small Step" and Wineskins — 154
12 – Perseverance During Tragedy — 157
13 – A Fre-Engine Red Water Pump — 160
14 – A Widow's Faith & Brian Masinick — 163
15 – Chickens and Fear — 165
16 – The English Teacher — 167

17 – Blind	169
18 – Seeking the Lost	172
19 – Christians Are Not Perfect	175
20 – Jesus	177
21 – Clown Communion	179
22 – "Jesus Christ Superstar!"	181
23 – Easter	184
24 – Now What?	186
25 – Now What? Conclusion	188
26 – Easter Faith	190
27 – 1-800-2Heaven	192
28 – Be Still?	195
29 – Be Still? Conclusion	197
30 – Going Fishing	199
31 – Going from Fishing to Ministry	201

Forward

Three small churches gathered by a pond to worship together. As we sang hymns and talked about Jesus preaching by the lake, we could look out on our own lake complete with fishing boat. I could picture Jesus standing in that boat just offshore as he speaks.

He tells a story about a farmer sowing seeds. According to the story, some of the seeds fell along the path and were eaten by birds. Some fell on rocky places. Some fell among thorns. But... some seed fell among good soil and produced a tremendous crop.

Such a simple story. What is Jesus teaching?

We live in turbulent times, full of tough days. At times we may feel frustrated, overwhelmed, and disconnected from each other and from God. We may wonder if Christ has anything to teach us as we face difficulties ahead.

Some days are like the seed on the path where good intentions are eaten up by the realities of daily living. Some days are like the seed that falls on rocky places where there is not time or space to do anything but survive. Some days are like the seed that falls among thorns where people and circumstances choke out all our best efforts.

But... some days, with a dose of God's encouragement can be full of blessings and opportunities that are multiplied many times over within your life and the lives of others. Jesus told a story that provided a dose of encouragement to help us face our tough days confident that we are not alone and there are better days ahead.

Standing out there among the crowd, the pond and the fishing boat gave me a wonderful perspective for how we absorb God's Word. A simple story about seeds teaches a life-giving message offering God's grace and encouragement.

Approximately thirty years ago, I visited the Amelia Bulletin Monitor newspaper office and suggested writing a weekly column. The owners, Mike and Ann Salster looked at me strangely and Ann said, "You know, we can't pay you." And so, my writing career began. The Salsters and I became close friends over the years as they published what I wrote every week and encouraged me to share the column with other newspapers and on websites. They provided expertise to start an internet devotion and prayer ministry and published four of my books. I will always be grateful for their enthusiastic support. Ann and Mike died years ago but their contribution to my ministry was huge.

"A Daily Dose of Godly Encouragement: Medicine for Tough Days" represents a summation of my attempts over the past thirty years to plant God's seeds of encouragement and hope within you. This book, "Winter" represents the first three months of a year-long opportunity to provide meaningful and transforming daily medicine.

There have been many doses of Godly encouragement planted in my life over the years. Some of those came from within my family and friends and some from the many churches I served. I am so grateful for the hundreds of people who have influenced and guided me.

My wife, Mell, stuck by my side all these years providing encouragement and love. My children, Stephen and his son, Jackson, my daughter Lisa and her husband Bobby and their son, Carson, my mother, Martha and my sister Kathy and her husband Greg have all been supportive.

I've served 12 churches and one district of 90 churches over the past thirty years, and they have all provided inspiration and encouragement. So many people have touched my life. Some of them appear in my stories but all of them made a difference in my life.

My prayer is that you will read and enjoy the daily doses of Godly encouragement, knowing that God wants to bless and inspire you. I pray you will use these stories as part of your devotional and prayer life and trust God to guide you from there.

I would love to hear from you. You can like one of my pages on Facebook. Larry Davies or Sowing Seeds of Faith or you can visit my website at www.SowingSeedsofFaith.org or email me at LarryDavies@PrayWithYou.org.

May God bless you richly on your faith journey.

Larry

January

January 1 – The Little Church that Could!

Matthew 7:24-29

Do you remember the children's book: "The Little Engine that Could?" A train full of toys could not get over the mountain to the children on the other side. What would they do? A shiny new engine was too good to help. A big engine would not bother. The rusty old engine was too tired. But a little blue engine replied, "I'm not very big, but I think I can. I think I can." Puff, puff, chug, chug, went the little blue engine. "I think I can."

"Hurray, hurray," cried the clown and all the toys. "The boys and girls in the city will be happy because you helped us." And the little blue engine seemed to say as she puffed steadily down the mountain. "I thought I could. I thought I could."

There is a world full of people who desperately need to know God loves them. What will we do? There are shiny new churches and large mega churches who do great and mighty works. But what about the many old little churches who are tempted to say: "I'm tired and discouraged! I can not. I can not."

Once upon a time, there was one old, little church, once vibrant and full of life. Two people joined a Bible

2

study where they expressed a need to open their little church to an after-school ministry: "With God's help," they said, "I think I can -- I think I can."

Soon, children were dropped off at the little church where they would be greeted with cookies, music, games and Bible study. Some of those children along with their parents began attending this same little church.

One man in the community nearly died. While in the hospital, he made a vow to serve God and come to this same little church. A mother brings her family to that little church looking for a fresh start. They become a source of inspiration and motivation.

A new Bible study starts, but this time the little church has its own class seeking ways to serve God. One woman persuades her family into joining the Bible study, while another woman begins teaching youth in the Sunday school. They form a choir.

"Hurray, hurray," cries this preacher and people everywhere as this little church puffs steadily on. And God replies: "Well done, good and faithful servant." The little church says: "With God's help, we thought we could -- we thought we could!"

With God's help, you can too!

Prayer Challenge: Old little churches who have lost hope.

January 2 – Resolutions & John the Baptist

Luke 3:1-14

One of my New Year's Resolutions every year is to get organized. I will buy a book, one or two check list pads, maybe a computer program all in hopes of organizing my life. Is the expense worth it? Not usually.

Michelle Singletary suggests four resolutions: "Resolve to mend broken relationships, become healthier, become more connected, resolve to help the poor."

But, if you ever want to meet someone who will tell you what he/she thinks, meet John the Baptist. If he were a preacher, he would be kicked out of every church. *"You brood of snakes! Who warned you to flee the coming wrath? Prove by the way you live you have repented of your sins and turned to God. Don't just say, 'We're safe, because we're good church members. That means nothing, God can create good church members from the dirt in this carpet."* (from Luke 3:7-8)

Do you feel warm and cherished? We don't like messages like this. Neither did the crowd listening to John the Baptist. None of us relish the idea of facing the reality of what we planted. That our apathy and our lifestyle can one day catch up to us. That's the bad news but there is help readily available. Even during

4

mistakes, mess-ups, bad choices and yes... sin, God loves us. God cares for us.

So, what do we do? We repent. When was the last time you got on your knees and said, "Oh, God, I'm going my own way. Forgive me." John the Baptist provides a blueprint: Share, be honest, be content. John is paving the way for Jesus who will get us off our knees and enable us to change. To understand forgiveness and grace, we must first understand our mistakes, mess-ups, bad choices and ultimately our sin.

Here is my resolution: "I resolve to deepen my relationship with God and anticipate miracles and not let fear hold me back." What usually holds us back from these kinds of serious commitments can be summed up by that one word: FEAR.

I discovered two interesting ways to express FEAR as an acrostic: Forget. Everything. And. Run. Or Face. Everything. And. Rise.

What choice will you make? Someone once said: "Christianity is not a religion. It is a relationship with God." How is your relationship? Resolve this year to deepen your relationship with God, anticipate miracles and don't let FEAR hold you back.

Prayer Challenge: Which FEAR will you choose? What are your resolutions?

January 3 – Aprons: A Symbol of Service

1 Peter 5:5-6

I learned something about aprons at DAIL Community near Seoul, South Korea. During the orientation we were given a bright orange apron by the founder, Rev. Choi known as the "Babfor" Pastor which means "pastor who scoops rice." We soon had our own "scoop rice" experience as hundreds of hungry people gathered to receive their meal. The work was tedious but gratifying. Very few of the people knew English, but it didn't stop them from smiling and bowing in appreciation.

Putting on an apron and serving others can seem monotonous and frustrating at times but the joy of helping someone can be immensely fulfilling. DAIL Community describes their purpose: "to practice God's commandment to love each other, spread the Good News to others and to live our lives like Jesus stretching out our hands to our abandoned neighbors creating a more beautiful world. It starts with anything; it starts with me; it starts now."

I passionately believe that God places opportunities in front of us every day. As these opportunities present themselves, we have a choice as to how we respond or don't respond. However, when we respond to the opportunities with faith, God often responds in miraculous ways.

At one point the DAIL Community was in deep financial distress. Food supplies were critically low while the number of people standing in line to receive meals grew substantially. Pastor Choi calculated that within two weeks the food would be gone and there were no funds to purchase more. Pastor Choi would no longer be able to serve the poor and the DAIL Community would collapse.

Pastor Choi had nothing left except faith in God and a life devoted to prayer.

That day, a large delivery truck pulled up in front of the center. The driver informed Pastor Choi that the company producing the noodles had experienced a recall that made it impossible for their company to sell an entire production run of noodles. They had no choice but to discard literally tons of food. The truck driver was told to deliver the entire quantity of recalled noodles to DAIL.

Each day, God offers opportunities to don aprons of humility and serve in a way that can be deeply gratifying. "Strengthen our weakness so that we may do better." Occasionally, God provides a miracle or two as a blessed reminder that we are never serving alone.

So, grab an apron and remember the words and lessons of Rev. Choi and the DAIL Community: "It starts with anything; it starts with me; it starts now."

Prayer Need: Help us recognize and respond to those in need around us.

January 4 – Anger & Grace

Matthew 18:21-35

I was standing in line, waiting for the store to open. The man behind me was wearing a mask. I asked if masks were still required. "Big mistake!" He started shouting theories as to why he would never take a vaccine and that progressed to a diatribe about a fraudulent election and current politicians and that led to an airliner secretly shot down by a Chinese missile.

I thought about sharing my opinion, but that would only provoke more angry outbursts. I found myself praying for the doors to open… soon.

The news is filled with stories of angry motorists, angry airline passengers, angry spectators at sporting events and politicians spouting accusations and conspiracy theories. Yet, the Bible teaches a very different attitude.

The Apostle Paul writes: "Be kind to each other, tenderhearted, forgiving one another, just as God through Christ has forgiven you." (Ephesians 4:32)

To be truly kind and tenderhearted we must first understand and model grace. Peter comes to Jesus and says, "Lord, how often shall my brother sin against me and I forgive him? Seven times?" (Mat. 18:21)

Seven times is generous, but Jesus responds with seventy times seven not as a number but as an attitude stressing, real forgiveness must be never-ending.

Jesus talks about a King forgiving someone a million dollars only to have that same person browbeat a fellow servant over twenty bucks. The King finds out and throws the scoundrel into prison to be tortured until he repays the debt. What is often left out or forgotten is the last line: "That's what my heavenly Father will do to you if you refuse to forgive from your heart."

Our churches and our faith are not taken seriously because we Christians are not all that different from the world around us. We seldom model Jesus, living a life of grace and forgiveness. I confess that forgiveness is hard for me. But I also believe a life of grace is our most effective witness to a deeply divided and angry world.

Prayer Challenge: Help us model kindness and an attitude of forgiveness.

January 5 – God and the Church

John 3:11-21

As we would say in the south, "I was raised right!" Being a navy family, we moved frequently so I went to many churches. I remember being in Christmas programs, singing in a children's choir. I also remember thinking worship was boring. My dad was no longer attending so why should I? In college, I could do what I wanted which did not include attending church. After college, my excuse was: "I work six days a week in a suit and tie. Why dress up on my only day off?"

I was among the many raised in church, exposed to the teachings of Jesus but chose to stay away. "I believed in God but didn't feel any need to be in church."

What changed me was "despite my outward successful appearances" there was a growing dissatisfaction with my current life and a question that haunted my conscious and unconscious thoughts: "Is this it? Is this all there is?" What also changed me was the growing realization that I needed to be in church on Sunday to get through the stress and strain of the other six days.

After becoming a pastor, I found this past experience gave me a deeper understanding of why others struggled not only with attending church but in their relationship with God.

"For this is how God loved the world: He gave his one and only Son, so that everyone who believes in him will not perish but have eternal life. God sent his Son into the world not to judge but to save the world through him." (John 3:16-17)

God loves us. He sacrificed His Son so that we have a path to follow and a companion to guide us through the twists and turns, bumps and bruises that are a part of our lives on earth.

Picture a wooden dock in winter stretching out to a thin shell of ice on the surrounding water. A young man walks out onto the dock reflecting on those lazy summer days. His sister shouts from the shoreline. Startled, he loses his balance on the slippery dock and crashes into the icy water. The quiet serenity of the scene has suddenly been replaced by icy reality.

In many ways, this describes what happens to us before we recognize our need for help, our need for others and our need for God. Everything is fine for a while, feet solidly planted on our own independence. Then something happens. It could be personal, or it could be something bigger. We lose our footing, and we go crashing into the pond. That is when we discover that we cannot be fully alive and navigate the slippery ice ahead of us without God.

Prayer Challenge: Enable me to help others find a deeper connection with God.

January 6 – Shoveling Snow

1 John 4:7-12

Our neighborhood was blasted with eighteen inches of snow. Everything was peaceful and quiet at first, but that ended when I went to shovel our driveway. I had a nifty tool called a snow slider that is fast and easy to use for two to three inches of snow but when pushed against this pile? Nothing moved. Sigh!

So, I grabbed a snow shovel and started digging. Did I mention there were eighteen inches of snow? I managed to clear a small path and took a break followed by more progress and another break. At this rate, I would be shoveling snow until July. Then, there was a knock on my door.

A neighbor had a snow blower never used. Today, he needed it and managed to clear his driveway within minutes. He had so much fun, he went over to help a neighbor. This neighbor was so grateful, he pitched in, and they both went to help someone else. Within a few hours, we had a cluster of houses with clean driveways. Happy neighbors were outside giving away cookies, coffee, and soup.

Often, our best witness as Christians is how we respond in a crisis. The neighbor who used his snow blower to clean people's driveways, accomplished more to demonstrate the love of Jesus then all the sermons I could preach. God often teaches a powerful lesson while doing a simple task. We could clear our own driveway but would likely finish feeling cranky and miserable. Instead, our neighbor displayed God's love in action.

I received this email: "I believe real church, real religion, happens in this church building and translates outside in our day-to-day encounters." The neighbor who used his snow blower to help a neighborhood was expressing God's love.

One of my favorite lessons from John Wesley is often called: The three simple rules. 1. Do no harm – by thought, word or action. 2. Do all the good you can – in building up the body of Christ and in loving and serving others and all of creation. Stay in Love with God – through Worship, Bible study, prayer, and good works.

God continually offers opportunities to witness our faith, sometimes through words and other times through actions. "If we love each other, God lives in us, and his love has been brought to full expression through us." 1 John 4:12

Prayer Challenge: How can you express God's love in tangible ways today?

January 7 – Prayer: Looking Within

Ephesians 6:10-20

"My Lord God I have no idea where I am going. I do not see the road ahead of me. I cannot know for certain where it will end. Nor do I really know myself, and the fact that I think I am following your will does not mean that I am actually doing so."

The writer of this prayer, Thomas Merton was a dedicated monk, who struggled with himself and with God. At times, he was uncertain about his calling. But that is what makes this prayer so profound. You identify with his struggle which prepares you to accept his solution.

"But I believe that my desire to please you does in fact please you. And I hope that I have that desire in all that I am doing. I hope that I will never do anything apart from that desire. And I know that if I do this you will lead me by the right road though I may know nothing about it."

The key word here is desire: His desire to please God in all that he is doing. His desire to walk in God's path even though at times he's unsure where that path will lead is one part of the solution.

"Therefore, I will trust you always though I may seem to be lost and in the shadow of death. I will not fear, for you are ever with me, and you will never leave me to face my perils alone."

Desire to please God leads to trust in God's plan to lead us through our life and faith challenges. He wants us to learn from what we experienced and use it to further spread His word, to be more faithful and to fully live by His example.

"Where are we going?" I'm not sure. "What is the road ahead?" I don't know.

Does this provide a sure-fire formula for surviving illness or change our deep-seated cultural and political divisions? No, but my desire to please God by surrendering my will to His control leads to trust in God to ultimately lead me in the right direction.

Prayer Challenge: Use Thomas Merton's prayer daily as a guide for 30 days.

January 8 – Winter Shelter

1 John chapter 4

Our church participated in housing 65 homeless guests for a week. We provided a place to sleep along with breakfast and dinner. My wife and I provided breakfast one morning. A local Bojangles offered to provide food and several volunteers joined in to serve. Dee Swanson, one of our volunteers wrote about what happened next:

When my husband and I arrived, the first thing we noticed was Pastor Larry talking to the Bojangles manager on the phone, "There is a fire, and you are not going to be able to bring anything? Oh no!" Immediately our volunteers began putting Plan B into action. Pastor Larry raced out to buy donuts. One volunteer rummaged through the freezer and found sausage and bacon. Others opened cans of fruit along with yogurt and muffins.

But then, after we delivered our makeshift breakfast? Surprise! Bojangles turned up with their promised menu. They had experienced a fire and were running behind. Whew! As the ad says, "It was Bo time!"

As I rolled one of the carts delivering the sausage biscuits, one of the guests asked, "Do you have any jam?" Without hesitation, I quickly responded, "No, we don't." At the same time, I was thinking to myself, "Hey, you have no idea how chaotic this morning has been. I just gave you a warm sausage biscuit. What more do you want?"

Obviously, what he wanted was simply some jam to go on the biscuit. Almost immediately, I could hear my mother's voice chastising me. "What a twerp you are! Did you forget that you are in God's house and supposedly sharing His love with these folks? You didn't even offer to go to the kitchen and look for jam?"

So, I stepped back and gave a second, more Christian response. "You know I'm new at this. Let me check." When I scurried into the kitchen, they found a cardboard box of at least 300 packets of jam plus another box of small butter containers. Now that's the way we show our Christian love: Warm sausage biscuits customized with jam and butter.

We are challenged to love our neighbor and offer God's love and grace as a testimony of our faith. One example? Providing shelter for our homeless guests. God is continually offering opportunities to witness our faith, sometimes through words and other times through actions. "If we love each other, God lives in us, and his love has been brought to full expression through us." (1 John 4:12)

Prayer Challenge: How can you share God's love with someone today?

January 9 – "Stairway to Heaven"

Matthew chapters 5-7

When the weather was warm on college campus during the seventies you often heard music blasting from open dorm windows. This song was one of them:

There's a lady who's sure all that glitters is gold
And she's buying a stairway to heaven...

"Stairway to Heaven" originated in 1970.Jimmy Page strummed the chords, and Robert Plant wrote the lyrics. There are lots of theories as to the meaning but according to the authors, it's more about shallow materialism and greed: "a woman getting everything she wanted without giving anything back." Our lady in the song is trying her best to buy her way through life yet there are choices: "There are two paths you can go by, but in the long run. There's still time to change the road you're on."

Your head is humming, and it won't go, in case you
don't know
The piper's calling you to join him
Dear lady, can you hear the wind blow, and did
you know
Your stairway lies on the whispering wind?

Here is where I get creative: You can't buy your way to heaven and your head is humming with confusion. But the piper's calling you to join him. Who is the piper? For me, it's Jesus, and he is calling. If you follow the Piper, your stairway to heaven will be guided by the whispering wind of God's Holy Spirit.

If Plant heard this, he would deny it, but I think it's an interesting way to interpret the song, especially when you understand what Jesus teaches. We are each on a stairway to heaven and Jesus is the piper calling us to join him.

As we climb the stairway to heaven, there are challenges along the way, but the song proclaims, "if you listen very hard, the tune will come to you at last. When all is one and one is all. That's what it is." Yes, there are two paths you can go by, but in the long run, there's still time to change the road you're on."

Finally, there is a plea: "Dear lady, can you hear the wind blow, and did you know your stairway lies on the whispering wind?" Ah but our lady doesn't choose to follow the piper or listen to the whispering wind. So, the final agonizing words of the song offer a final dirge: "And she's buying a stairway to heaven."

That is her choice, but it doesn't have to be yours. There is a better way.

Prayer Challenge: We all have choices. What choices to you need to make today?

January 10 – Cat-Kicking
(Based on a story by Zig Ziglar)

1 Peter 3:8-11

The steering wheel was never gripped tighter as Jim, the owner of a local automobile dealership drove to work. Early that morning his wife forcefully exclaimed: "I can't take your workaholic ways anymore. We're through. If you don't learn to spend more time with me and your family, we're leaving, forever!"

Jim stomped to his office, slammed the door, smacked the intercom button on his telephone and shouted for his sales manager: "Larry, come to my office now!"

Larry was a first-rate manager, but sales were off. "Larry, I'm tired of your poor production and pitiful excuses. I expect you to whip our staff into shape. If you can't, then I'll hire someone who can. Do you hear me?!"

"Yes sir." What else could Larry say? Plenty, as he walked out mumbling: "That no good, sorry excuse for an owner! Where does he get off threatening me after I've worked so hard for him? We've seen rougher times. What a jerk!"

Larry barged into the office of Robin his top sales rep: "I'm tired of making you look good. You would be nothing if I wasn't handing you sales. If you don't do better, I'm replacing you with a real salesperson. Do you understand?!!"

Robin understood. "He has a lot of nerve jumping on me after all the sales I've generated. The only reason he became a manager is because of me!" Just then, the phone rang. Robin shouted at the receptionist: "Hold all my calls! If you were any kind of decent receptionist, you would know that I'm busy! Just remember -- you too can be replaced!"

"Well, the nerve of that prima donna!" thought the receptionist. "Who does she think she is?" For the rest of the day, when anyone called, instead of, "How can I help you?" The unfortunate caller was met with a gruff, "What do you want?"

When the receptionist finally made it home, she walked in on her son lying on the couch watching TV. "Son, how many times have I told you that you need to carry more weight. This room is a disgusting mess. How dare you watch television when I work all day like a slave! Go to your room. You're grounded -- for life!"

The boy hopped from the couch and stomped toward his room. On the way, he noticed Ellis, the family cat asleep on the floor. Before the poor critter could utter a decent meow, the boy gave poor Ellis a vicious kick.

Question: Wouldn't Jim, the car dealer, avoid a lot of trouble if he just went to the receptionist's house and kicked the cat himself? Another question: Who's been kicking your cat? Whose cat have you kicked? Stay tuned for answers tomorrow.

January 11 – Cat-Kicking Answers

1 Peter 3:8-11

In yesterday's story, Jim, the car dealer could have avoided a lot of trouble if he just went to the receptionist's house and kicked the cat himself. Question: Who's been kicking your cat? Whose cat have you kicked? We live in a negative cat-kicking world full of failures, disappointments, back-biting and plain-old meanness. None of us are immune.

To deal with the frustrations we need extraordinary patience and courage. In his letter to the Philippians, Paul wrote: "I learned the secret of living in every situation. For I can do everything with the help of Christ who gives me the strength I need." Wouldn't you love to have that kind of contentment? How can we learn to respond like Paul, with gentleness and grace?

Well, here is what you should **not** do!

- Don't look for another cat to kick. That's abuse.
- Don't whine to everyone you know. That's gossip.
- Don't throw a temper tantrum. That's immature.
- Don't take your ball and go home. That's quitting.
- Don't use the silent treatment. That's weak.
- Don't vow to get even. That's revenge.
- Yet, doing nothing won't work. That's unhealthy for them and for you.

How can you and I apply Paul's words? "I can do anything with the help of Christ." How do we do that? One answer comes from Peter. (1 Peter 3:8-11)

- "Be of one mind, full of sympathy." Pray for guidance.
- "Don't repay evil for evil. Don't retaliate." Fight the urge to get even.
- "Pay them back with a blessing." Instead, show kindness.
- "God will bless you." Perspective reminds you are serving God.
- "Keep your tongue from speaking evil." Avoid complaining.
- "Turn away from evil and do good." Look to set a good example.
- "Work hard at living in peace with others." Living in peace is hard work.

If we apply this, here is how the cat-kicking story should end: Jim apologized to his wife and promised to be a better husband and father. He also apologized for taking his frustration out on Larry. Larry sought out Robin and asked forgiveness for being so rude. Robin brought cookies to the receptionist and apologized for her behavior. The receptionist brought pizza home and promised to be a more understanding mother. As for Ellis the cat? He received extra treats that week.

Prayer Challenge: How can we deal with frustrations and encourage one another?

January 12 – $10 Challenge

Matthew 25:14-30

A church giving away $10 bills? Whoever heard of such a thing? Especially when most churches are having stewardship campaigns to raise more money, not give it away!

"My wife and I know a waitress who recently had surgery and is the sole support for her husband (disabled) and 2 sons. We gave her a $20 tip."

Jesus told this parable: "The Master called together his servants and gave them money to invest for him while he was gone." (Matthew 25:14)

"I'm a 10-year-old kid who took the money you gave me and added my six dollars allowance to buy food for the pantry at our church."

Why would Jesus talk about giving money to three employees to invest? Two of them doubled their investment and received praise. But the third hid the money and returned what was given. The boss became angry and fired him.

The lesson? To those who use well what they are given, even more will be given, and they will have an abundance. But from those who do nothing, even what little they have will be taken away. (Mat. 25:29)

One finance committee member said, "I can't wait to see the look on their faces when they see we are giving them money! What kind of church does that?"

"I decided to discuss it with our 3 sons. We purchased 20 boxes of cereal for the food pantry restock drive at school, however, it quickly turned into a competition. When the other students saw them carrying in 20 boxes of cereal they gave generously too."

What were the results? Numerous acts of kindness and increased awareness that even a small amount of money, used with creativity and prayer can make a huge difference! Practicing extravagant generosity can be life changing for the giver as well as the receiver! Not a bad lesson for $10.

"My little boy wanted to use our $10 to buy the church a dog. He said the Pastors could take care of it. We didn't do that!"

Prayer Challenge: Help me use my resources more creatively to help others.

January 13 – $10 Challenge Stories

2 Corinthians 9:6-15

One Sunday, each family received a $10 bill with a challenge to multiply and use it in a way that would help someone or some organization and write about their experience.

My goal was to find a way to give back that required giving of myself in addition to anything monetary. Friday night dinner is always a visit to a local restaurant. I often see an elderly gentleman who sits alone. I was told, his wife recently died. I paid for his dinner before but next time I see him I will pay for his dinner and introduce myself. I cannot imagine being old, alone, and eating by yourself.

The gift of a tree is a gift to future generations. The value of a single tree may be insignificant, but each tree gives us air to breathe, shade to cool, roots to stabilize the soil and prevent erosion, habitat for God's creatures and beauty to treasure and cherish.

I went to the grocery store, purchased two chickens and made 2 pot pies for an elderly gentleman and also for a neighbor home from the hospital. With the left-over chicken, I delivered chicken salad to a friend with a note that said" I'm praying for you, today!

I bought a book of stamps and mailed out the following poem to my friends:

In the quiet of your home with the Bible on your knee,
I invite you to share in a wonderful cup of tea
Please be my honored guest at this marvelous special tea
And remember all the others not as fortunate as we
With a special goal in mind, we hope you will agree
To send us a thoughtful gift, to help those in poverty.

I received over $500 to help others in need.

Paul wrote: You must each decide in your heart how much to give. And don't give reluctantly or in response to pressure. For God loves a person who gives cheerfully. And God will generously provide all you need. Then you will always have everything you need, and plenty left over to share with others. (2 Cor. 9:7-8)

If God can multiply $10 into so many creative and helpful ministries, just think what God can do with you and your talents and resources.

Prayer Challenge: How can God use you and your resources for ministry?

January 14 – More $10 Challenge

Luke 6:38

One Sunday, each family received a $10 bill with a challenge to multiply and use it in a way that would help someone or some organization and write about their experience.

At an event helping refugees, several women brought toys for the children. Watching their faces light up with things as simple as crayons and stuffed animals was incredible. These families LITERALLY left their country with nothing but the clothes they had on. I walked away overwhelmed and warmed. I got to researching and found an organization set up to support refugees resettling. My $10 was joined by a few more bills.

I added to the $10 and gave three young men ages 11, 12 and 13 a challenge to do something good with it. One gave a book to his school library. Another contributed something to his band class. One made pet beds for the animal shelter.

Several times, we purchased things we could live without: The occasional dinner out or an item we wanted but didn't truly need. So, we came up with occasions when we should have been more mindful of our choices. If we have the choice to buy a burger, we also have the better choice to use that money to help others. This was a great reminder to look beyond ourselves with open hearts, gratefulness, and humility.

I found out a friend lost her leg. She could no longer work and had no medical insurance. With a prayer, a GoFundMe page was set up. I began sharing on Facebook, posting info everywhere. The newspaper wrote an article. My friend was overwhelmed and so appreciative of the donations and cards she received. The GoFundMe page raised approximately $12,000.

Jesus said: "Give, and you will receive. Your gift will return to you in full—pressed down, shaken together to make room for more, running over, and poured into your lap. The amount you give will determine the amount you get back." (Luke 6:38)

$10 given, pressed down, shaken together to make room for more, running over and poured into ministry and sprinkled with faith creates miracles.

Prayer Challenge: Help me better use my resources to serve God.

January 15 – A Tornado and Two Churches

Hebrews 13:15-16

It was a quiet Sunday afternoon. Suddenly, the skies grew dark, the wind blew fiercely, and we were bombarded by hail. Then it was over. The news flash said a tornado touched down within two miles of our home.

The next morning our newspaper featured an article about the destruction of Lawyers Missionary Baptist Church by the same tornado. The picture showed a church with both side walls and roof blown away. Yet, you could plainly see the exposed pews with bibles and hymnals still in the racks.

I couldn't take my eyes off the picture. An inner voice kept asking: "What will they do next Sunday? Where will they go? This church is only a few miles away. Surely, we can do something but what?"

Our church was building a new worship area. The current sanctuary was too small, so we met in the gym at the other end of the building. This church desperately needed a sanctuary. We had it. We weren't using it. How can we possibly say no? Actually, there were plenty of reasons.

We have limited parking available and couldn't handle extra cars. They are Baptist and we are Methodist. Their congregation is mostly black and ours is mostly white. But the inner voice kept on: "Suppose this was your church. Wouldn't you want someone to help you?"

I called and met with Rev. Carlton Johnson of Lawyers Missionary Baptist Church that morning and stood in the sanctuary among the exposed pews and tried to imagine what force of nature could possibly cause this much damage. You could see the concern and hurt in his eyes. "Rev. Johnson," I heard myself saying, "We have a church sanctuary, and we would be delighted to have you join us."

The following Sunday, two congregations met as one church. In the hallway connecting the two sanctuaries were tables filled with food and coffee. As members of their church arrived, people from our church were there to greet them. Several members volunteered to attend their worship service to show support.

Were there any comments? Yes, there were:

- We need a joint covered dish supper so we can get to know each other.
- How can we help raise money for their new church?
- Would they like to combine with our youth program or our Bible studies?

My favorite comment however was made by more than one of our members: "I have never been so proud to be a member of this church."

Prayer Challenge: Help me become more aware of the needs all around me?

January 16 – 1 Tornado, 2 Churches = One New Church Building

Galatians 5:6-10

Darrell Laurant, a local columnist wrote: "As movie reviewers love to say, this is the feel-good story of the year." For several years, our two churches shared the same building and more. There were concerts and dinners to raise money. There were joint worship services. The youth groups were involved in mission projects. But there seemed to be little progress toward rebuilding Lawyers Missionary Baptist Church.

Then along came a $10 stewardship challenge. The challenge was to see what you could do to make ten bucks grow. Jim Adams, a local contractor, and church member stood up and said: "For my $10 challenge, I'm going to rebuild Lawyers Missionary Baptist Church." You could have heard a pin drop; it was so quiet.

A local company donated a stained-glass window. Another company installed heating and air-conditioning free. Most of the building supplies were donated. One church donated a baptismal pool. Another church donated pews and raised money to buy their new steeple. Hundreds of volunteers worked on the building or supplied food.

Pastor Carlton Johnson said, "I'm excited and overjoyed. We've been looking forward to this day and praying. This is the day the Lord has made," he added, "this is bringing people together, black and white, Baptist and Methodist. It's wonderful."

At the first worship service inside the new church building, Jim Adams, the builder who led and organized the rebuilding of Lawyers Missionary Baptist Church stood before Rev. Johnson and announced their building was finished and debt-free. Then Jim presented the original $10 that started this amazing miracle.

Today, if you visit Lawyers Missionary Baptist Church in Lynchburg, Virginia you will find a framed $10 bill hung on their wall and if you ask, they will happily tell you the story of how one tornado brought two churches together to accomplish one incredibly awesome miracle.

Prayer Challenge: Help me have the courage to follow where God leads me.

January 17 – Brokenness to Reconciliation

Matthew 5:23-26

A few minutes into our visit she began to weep. *"I'm so sorry."* For the next hour, I heard a sad story of mistakes, misunderstandings and family disagreements. None of them seemed all that serious, but her speech was tortured with words of guilt and hurt. *"Will God ever forgive me?"* she asked. We talked of God's healing comfort and grace and studied Bible passages. Finally, we said a prayer together with her asking God for forgiveness. All in all, it was exactly what a pastor should do on a visit. I felt satisfied.

Months later, on our second visit, she began to weep and the same sad story began. Just like before, her speech was tortured with words of guilt and hurt. We talked again of God's healing comfort and grace and studied the appropriate Biblical passages. We said a prayer together. It was exactly what a pastor should do on a visit. But I knew something was wrong.

Jesus spoke about forgiveness, but he also spoke about reconciliation, which means making adjustments in a difficult relationship. You cannot reconcile without getting actively involved and making compromises. One reason the woman suffered was because she expected

God to wave a magic wand of forgiveness without active participation from her.

I visited a third time armed with newfound knowledge. Again, she began to weep and tell her sad story. But this time, I interrupted and began to talk about what God's gift of healing meant. At first, she looked as if I had lost my mind, but didn't stop me. After a moment we prayed and I left having no idea what would happen.

Months later, during a family gathering, she was given the opportunity to tell her story. It wasn't easy, but after hours of talking and crying, years of misunderstandings and deep hurts were brought into the open and over time God's wonderful grace began to heal a broken and deeply divided family.

On a later visit, after a few moments, she began to laugh. *"So much has changed!"* For the next hour, I heard about family gatherings and exploits of wayward grandchildren. Her speech was animated with words of hope. For another few minutes we talked about community and church concerns. Finally, we said a prayer together.

All in all, it was exactly what a pastor should do. I felt enormously thankful.

Prayer Challenge: Who needs to move from brokenness to reconciliation?

January 18 – Pandemic Memories

Colossians 3:12-17

Anonymous posting on Facebook in 2020 during the Pandemic:

- The dumbest thing I ever bought was a 2020 planner.
- I called Jake from State Farm just to talk. He asked what I was wearing.
- Old folks are sneaking out and their kids are yelling at them to stay in!
- Try your jeans on to be sure they fit. Pajamas will have you believe all is well.
- "I wouldn't touch him/her with a 6-foot pole" has become national policy!
- I need to practice social distancing from the refrigerator.
- I never imagined I would go to a bank wearing a mask and ask for money.

Before COVID, kids sat side by side in classrooms, adults crowded around tables in restaurants, sports fans packed into stadiums. Going to the office meant, well, going to the office. Attending church meant driving to a church building. Face masks were worn in hospitals. The Pandemic saw so many changes in the way we live and in how we regard our community and our institutions, including the church.

Since then, society has become even more polarized. Cultural and political clashes deepened. People increasingly select sources of news and information to reinforce their own views, often insulating themselves from those who think differently.

When it comes to the church, people are suspicious, resistant, and even hostile. For many: the church is irrelevant and unrelated to their daily lives. Yet, during the pandemic, church leaders often responded with creativity and faith, with perseverance rather than panic. We felt challenged but trusted in God's guidance.

Since God chose you to be the holy people he loves. (Col 3:12) Paul is speaking to us as the church. We are chosen, especially for times such as these.

Clothe yourselves with tenderhearted mercy, kindness, humility, gentleness, and patience. Make allowance for each other's faults and forgive anyone who offends you. Clothe yourselves with love, which binds us all together in perfect harmony. And let the peace that comes from Christ rule in your hearts. For as members of one body, you are called to live in peace. And always be thankful. (Col. 3:13-15)

This passage perfectly describes how we should model our behavior if we intend to be influential in the world around us, especially in times of crisis. How we act, what we say and how we respond will effectively communicate what kind of Christians we are and what our church ultimately stands for.

Prayer Challenge: Help us be the holy people of God for others.

January 19 – Monopoly

Mark 10:13-16

Monopoly replaced three of their tokens. I grew up playing with those pieces. I like the wheelbarrow best of all. The new pieces are T-Rex, a rubber ducky, and a penguin. Can you believe it? An obvious attempt to reach young people. Well, I say, let the young people get their own game.

"One day some parents brought their children to Jesus so he could touch and bless them. But the disciples scolded the parents for bothering him." And they should scold those parents. Jesus is busy. He should not be disturbed. Right?

But, when Jesus saw what was happening, he was angry. He said, "Let the children come to me. Don't stop them! For the Kingdom of God belongs to those who are like these children. I tell you the truth, anyone who doesn't receive the Kingdom of God like a child will never enter it." Then he took the children in his arms and placed his hands on their heads and blessed them.

Several fifth graders at our church were given the opportunity to answer the question: "What do I know about God?"

- "I am here to tell you what I know about God, but if you're wondering why, it's because ADULTS MAKE THINGS SO COMPLICATED."
- "My sister had heart problems and needed surgery. I was scared so I asked God to be with her. She is okay and back to her annoying self."
- "God loves us very much. He will always love us. There is nothing I can do to make God quit loving me. That is so cool!"
- "God makes miracles happen. God answers prayer and has a purpose for everything even if we don't understand."

Our children can teach us. There will always be change, but Jesus Christ will be with us no matter what. He will be with us as we change Monopoly pieces, grow older, change jobs and throughout all of life's changes. Jesus will be there.

That's a promise from God whether you are young or old.

Prayer Challenge: Help us learn from as well as teach our children.

January 20 – Instrument of Peace

Matthew 5:1-12

*Lord, make me an instrument of your peace: where
there is hatred, let me sow love;
where there is injury, pardon; where there is doubt,
faith; where there is despair, hope; where there is
darkness, light; where there is sadness, joy.*

This anonymous prayer called the Prayer of Saint
Francis or Peace Prayer seems especially appropriate
during times of crisis. Peace is desperately needed
amidst deep political and cultural divisions. Jesus said:
*"God blesses those who work for peace, for they will be
called the children of God."* (Mat. 5:9)

The church can and should play an important role in
healing conflict, but churches face their own divisions
and difficulties. Jesus calls us to be peace makers
during times of crisis. In fact, our ability to work for and
encourage peace could be the most important witness
we present to the world. So how do we do that? The
Peace Prayer continues:

*O divine Master, grant that I may not so much seek
to be consoled as to console, to be understood as
to understand, to be loved as to love. For it is in
giving that we receive, it is in pardoning that we*

are pardoned, and it is in dying that we are born to eternal life.

How do we work for peace? We learn to move from selfish to selfless. We move away from constantly seeking consolation, trying to be understood, maneuvering to be loved and move toward consoling others, understanding others, and loving others. When we learn to give, we receive far more. When we learn to forgive, we truly feel forgiven.

As the church: We present a testimony of "Godly Peace" within our community and world as we also provide a safe sanctuary of encouragement allowing differences of opinion to be worked out peacefully. We model "Godly Peace" to the outside world.

I read of a pastor who whenever eating in a restaurant, said to the server: "When you bring the food, we're going to have a prayer. If there is anything, you'd like us to pray for, let me know." Almost always, the server asked for prayers for a child, a friend, or a parent. Most were touched by the offer. Often servers would speak with him as he was leaving and ask, "How did you know I needed prayer?"

"Lord, make me an instrument of your peace."

Prayer Challenge: Lord, teach me to be an instrument of your peace.

January 21 – Ten "Old Testament" Action Words

Joshua 24:14-16

To be spiritually healthy, we heed the warnings of the Bible. What is the warning? Don't stop doing the good things that brought you to this point. Here are ten action words, I believe describe a healthy spiritual attitude. The words cry out: "Don't Stop!"

1. **Praise** – "To all who mourn, he will give beauty for ashes, joy instead of mourning and praise instead of despair." (Isaiah 61:3) Praise is submitting to God's authority.

2. **Prayer** – "He went home and knelt down as usual in his upstairs room and prayed." (Daniel 6:10) Prayer is our willingness to listen for God.

3. **Open** – "Then the Lord told Abram, "Leave your country! I will make you a blessing to others. (Genesis 12:1-4) Listening to God's voice often requires change.

4. **Hospitality** – "You welcome me as a guest, anointing my head with oil." (Psalm 23:5) Hospitality has to be more than a smile and polite, "How are you?"

5. **Obedient** – "The people said to Joshua, "We will serve the Lord our God. We will obey." (Joshua 24:24)

We are called to be obedient to God's purpose for our lives.

6. **Alert** – "Intelligent people are always open to new ideas. In fact, they look for them." (Proverbs 18:15) Are we alert to opportunities available?

7. **Assertive** – Will we aggressively with faith pursue those opportunities? "Don't worry about a thing," David told Saul. "I'll go fight Goliath." (1 Samuel 17:32)

8. **Risk** – Every opportunity also has a cost. Are you willing to pay? "God will rescue us but even if he doesn't, we will never serve your gods." (Daniel 3:17-18)

9. **Persistent** – Will we hang in there when the going gets tough? "Look! I am going to breathe into you and make you live again! (Ezekiel 37:5)

10. **Thankful** – Do we give thanks to the One who is so critical to our success? "Enter His gates with thanksgiving; go into his courts with praise." (Psalm 100:4)

Ten Old Testament action words to describe our desired response to God's teaching and grace.

Prayer Challenge: How can these ten action words impact your future?

January 22 – Three Emails

Ephesians 4:25-32

Three emails came at various times. Each writer expresses, a need to connect with God, to be forgiven and receive a fresh start.

"It has been 15 years since my first abortion. I have been coming to terms with my past and it scares me. I remember the first one vividly. I remember the date, sights and sounds and smell. The other two, I have no memory at all. I need help with forgiveness, but it is a daily struggle."

After a person experiences abortion, there often follows a lifetime of what ifs, grief, guilt, shame, and regrets.

"I am sitting here with tears streaming down my face, thankful to Jesus after hours of surfing the net and typing 'Christian & Divorce.' Perhaps my best bet would be to drive my car over a bridge rather than face the rest of my life as a divorced Christian woman. I read about your divorce recovery and God caused a tiny glimmer of hope to rise in me. I am hurting so badly because like many Christians, I never believed this would happen to me. I just need to know that Jesus can take the ashes of my life and restore me. Please pray for me."

Divorce is never the end. Divorce recovery can lead to restoration.

"I am the teacher who stumbled upon your website. I asked you to pray that I would find my way to God. Thanks to your website, I received at least a dozen responses. I never expected to have people write and try to help me. The support and advice given to me by complete strangers was nothing short of miraculous. I am learning the value of "praying without ceasing," and I am beginning to develop a relationship with God and Jesus. Thank you."

A teacher desperately searches for hope and faith and people respond. Many shared their own struggles and how God answered in miraculous ways.

Life is full of mistakes, sorrows, difficulties, obstacles and disappointments. Yet through it all, I discovered story after story of God working miracles, saving lives, touching hearts, and mending souls.

Prayer: Thank you for your continuing response to those seeking faith and hope.

January 23 – "Stop! Hey, What's that Sound?"

Nehemiah 1 & 2

The song was a sixties hit, "For What It's Worth" by Buffalo Springfield. Stephen Stills wrote it as part of a youth protest of anti-loitering laws in California, but today, those same words could easily apply to many of today's problems.

"There's something happening here, but what it is ain't exactly clear. There's battle lines being drawn. Nobody's right if everybody's wrong." The last verse offers a warning: "Paranoia strikes deep. Into your life it will creep. It starts when you're always afraid."

Those words still apply: There's something happening here can represent conflicts, natural disasters, financial crisis. Battle lines being drawn could be about red versus blue, gay versus straight, white versus black.

Everybody's talking but no one's listening. The result? "Paranoia strikes deep. Into your life, it will creep. It starts when you're always afraid."

The chorus is what our response should be: "It's time we stop. Hey, what's that sound? Everybody look, what's going down?" Stop giving-in to the maddening swirl of events. Tone down the noise of non-stop news and opinions. Look at what is going on around you with eyes of faith.

"There's something happening here" occurred with Nehemiah, when he received news that the wall surrounding, Jerusalem was down and the city was in ruins.

Nehemiah needed to stop and look at what was going down with the community he loved so he did what any Godly leader must do: he looked, he wept and then he prayed. "When I heard this, I sat down and wept. In fact, for days I mourned, fasted, and prayed to the God of heaven." (Nehemiah 1:4)

In the midst of his prayer God gave Nehemiah a bold plan to help his community build the wall they desperately needed. Three things happened:

1. Prayer – Nehemiah took the time to confess and listen to God.
2. Vision – He came up with a vision that made the next steps worthwhile.
3. Communicate – Nehemiah convinced his King and his community to join.

Nehemiah not only let go of the past, he took a community with him and began the huge task of rebuilding the wall around Jerusalem.

"You gotta stop. Hey, what's that sound. Everybody look, what's going down."

Prayer Challenge: "Stop, hey what's that sound. Look what's going down."

January 24 – Stumbling

Job 1 & 2

For a children's message I said, "At any time, your calm and reasonable life can be disrupted. We stumble and fall!" So, to make my point, I deliberately stumbled down the steps fully intending to catch myself. Somehow, I lost my balance in the act of falling and hit the floor, hard. In my enthusiasm to make a point, I nearly ruined the service and one of my knees in the process.

Despite my clumsiness, stumbling is an unfortunate element of life. At any time:

- The doctor asks to see you in her office to discuss a recent biopsy.
- Your employer schedules an appointment. There are rumors of layoffs.
- Your spouse confesses he/she is unfaithful and wants out of the marriage.
- A sleepy driver runs a stop sign directly in front of you.

You ask: "What do I do? How could this happen? What went wrong?" Your world becomes a blur as you spin out of control. The pavement underneath your feet that seemed so firm and sure has unexpectedly shifted and you stumble.

The best Biblical example of stumbling is the story of Job, a prosperous farmer described as "the finest man in all the earth – a man of complete integrity." But before you can say "stumble," Job, through no fault of his own loses his possessions, his family and even his health until he is left sitting on an ash heap scrapping his itching, boil covered skin with a broken piece of pottery.

Job cries out to God proclaiming his innocence while his so-called friends offer explanations: "Maybe, you did something wrong? Could it be your children's fault? Somebody must have done something wrong! You are simply being disciplined. Don't be angry with God! Shut up; you have no right to complain."

Whoa! With friends like this, who needs… friends.

But don't be smug. Job's friends represent our own well-meaning response when people around us suddenly find themselves stumbling. Instead of compassion, you offer cheap explanations. Instead of help, I offer unwanted criticism. Instead of empathy we offer slanderous gossip. Meanwhile Job, confused and even angry at times continues crying out to almighty God…

Job cries out: *"If only someone would listen to me! I will sign my name to my defense. Let the Almighty answer me. Let my accuser write out the charges against me. I would face the accusation proudly. I would wear it like a crown."*

Just when you think all is lost: "The Lord answers Job from the whirlwind."

Next: Job (Chapters) 1 and 2 meets God. Meanwhile – Read prayerfully Job 1 & 2

January 25 – Stumbling and Job

Job Chapters 38 & 42

Job stumbles! Just when all seems lost: "The Lord answers from the whirlwind."

"Brace yourself because I have some questions for you. Where were you when I laid the foundation of the earth? Who defined the boundaries of the sea? Have you ever commanded the morning to appear? Where does the light come from? Can you hold back the movements of the stars?" (Parts of Job 38)

Sounds impressive but now I have more questions than answers. Job was asking, "Where were you when I was suffering?" God answers, "Where were you when I created the earth?"

What? "What kind of answer is that?" It may be the best answer of all because Job comprehends who God really is. "I know you can do anything, and I was talking about things I did not understand, things too wonderful for me. I take back everything I said." (42:2-3) Wait a minute. What did Job suddenly understand?

At the beginning of Job there is a mysterious conversation between God and Satan. God brags about Job but Satan replies: "Yes, Job fears God, but not without good reason! You have always protected him but take away everything he has, and he will surely curse you!" (1:9-11)

All the forces of good and evil are watching. How would Job respond? We see him cry for mercy, beg for answers, and scream from the pain but when God finally appears? What will Job do? We expect him to curse and complain. But instead, Job chooses to trust God and because of his courage and faith, all of heaven celebrates as evil is defeated.

- When the doctor calls... can you trust God to see you through?
- When you lose your job... can you believe something better is waiting?
- When your spouse abandons you... can you believe God is ever faithful?
- When a car pulls in front of you... can you believe God is still in control?

Studying Job fortifies your faith and strengthens an attitude that is part trust and part perseverance. Sudden storms appear out of nowhere. You will stumble from time to time. The question is: "How will you respond when you stumble and fall? What attitude will you choose?"

All of heaven and hell is watching...

Prayer Challenge: How can understanding Job strengthen your faith?

January 26- Comfort

2 Corinthians 1:3-7

I searched for the word "comfort" in a Bible on my computer. In seconds, there were over 60 verses. I printed five pages of scripture and shared them at our Bible study. Each person was asked to pick a verse and share it with the class.

"*Even though I walk through the valley of the shadow of death, I will fear no evil, for you are with me; your rod and your staff, they comfort me.*" (Psalm 23:4) Mary talked of her father dying and how hearing those words at the funeral reminded her of Dad's loving protection and discipline.

"*I have seen his ways, but I will heal him; I will guide him and restore comfort to him…*" (Isaiah 57:18) John laughed and said, "God knows what kind of rascal I am, and He still offers healing and comfort!"

Two women spoke of Ruth 2:13: "*May I continue to find favor in your eyes, my Lord. You have given me comfort and have spoken kindly to your servant -- though I do not have the standing of one of your servant girls.*" They spoke of receiving love and comfort from their church family during difficult times.

Greg became excited when he found this one. "*My comfort in my suffering is this: Your promise preserves my life."* (Psalm 119:50) He had been going through a painful marital separation and was looking for direction in his life. He found the comfort of God that night and eventually discovered the strength to begin putting his life back together.

Jennifer shared: *"May your unfailing love be my comfort, according to your promise to your servant."* (Psalm 119:76) Her children had been difficult that day as she began to cry. Across the table someone quietly read another verse to her. *"As a mother comforts her child, so I will comfort you…"* (Isaiah 66:13)

You could feel God's Holy Spirit in the room offering reassurance as God's Word began to soothe troubled hearts and quiet frayed nerves. Tears of sorrow were replaced by sighs of relief as our class members experienced the compassion and the love of a God who never fails to offer comfort, even in the most difficult of circumstances.

What crisis have you been experiencing lately? Have you lost a loved one? Are you worried over your children? Are you struggling with financial or medical problems? There are verses of comfort. Just open your Bible and read. Before long you will feel the power of God and the words of comfort will flood the depths of your soul.

The Bible Study ended with a reminder from Isaiah: *"Comfort, comfort my people, says your God."* (40:1)

Prayer Challenge: How has God provided comfort for you?

January 27 – Three Funerals

Galatians 5:22-23

There was a picture of an older woman holding a child. The caption read: "One day you'll be just a memory for some people. Do your best to be a good one." Now that I am older and retired, I have been thinking about memories.

Senator John McCain asked Barak Obama and George W. Bush, from two different political parties, who each bested him in a Presidential election, to give the eulogies at his funeral. This symbolizes what I admire about Senator McCain: an ability to forgive and move on, always looking to a brighter future.

At another funeral, the supervisor for a nursing home where a pastor lived the last few months of his life talked of the love and respect she felt: "He had such a kind smile. I found myself drawn to him. When days became difficult, I frequently visited his room just to be nearby. I didn't even know he was a minister at first. I just knew that he had a comforting glow that somehow helped me feel loved by God."

At another funeral for a pastor, there were people from each of the churches she served. One spoke with pride of how lives were changed because of her ministry.

Mostly they talked about ministries in the community which are still active today.

A willingness to forgive. A comforting glow. Involvement in something that lives on.

"But the Holy Spirit produces this kind of fruit in our lives: love, joy, peace, patience, kindness, goodness, faithfulness, gentleness, and self-control. There is no law against these things!" - Galatians 5:22-23

Our devotion to modeling God's fruit: love, joy, peace, patience, kindness, goodness, faithfulness, gentleness and self-control makes it easier to focus more on our relationship with God and less on the hurts inflicted on us. Modeling God's fruit consistently day by day produces a comforting glow that draws others and encourages reaching out in ministry to others that results in changed lives.

"One day you'll be just a memory for some people. Do your best to be a good one."

Prayer Challenge: How can we better live a life bearing good fruit?

January 28 – Prayer for a Dead Church

Ezekiel 37

I dreamed God placed me in a church. I walked up and down the aisle among lots of people. They all looked – gulp – they all looked dead! There were children with crayons in their hands, teenagers sitting among friends, mothers cradling babies and choir members holding music. God asked: "Preacher, can these dead people live?"

This is my modernization of Ezekiel 37: "Valley of Dry Bones." Ezekiel asks: "Can these dead people live?" Or as I say: "Can today's church still make a difference?"

God said: *"Preach to these dead people and say, 'Hear the word of the Lord! I will breathe into your bodies, and you will come to life. You will smile at one another. You will welcome strangers, visit the sick and volunteer to help the helpless."*

Can God still breathe life into the church? Ezekiel continues: *"So I preached to the dead people. First one person began to smile and then another moved his head. One woman folded her hands together as if in prayer but there was still no twinkle of light in any of their eyes or color in their cheeks."*

People are searching for a faith community that is authentic and alive. They desire a deeper spiritual life. They are open to experiencing God and want to be part of something that matters, something compelling, a true faith community.

"So, I did as God commanded and there were strange noises throughout the congregation as people began first to breathe, then to sing, not like dead people, but with the excitement of folks possessed by God's living spirit."

One man in the midst of a painful marital separation shouted, "God healed me!" Another left the church to seek a former friend and reconcile their differences. One elderly woman walked over to the youth and offered hugs. A woman was led to donate a portion of her profits toward a homeless shelter.

Ezekiel goes on to say: *"These dead bodies represent my beloved church whose hope for living is gone. Therefore, preach to them and say: 'God promises to open your graves and give you life. I will put my Spirit in you, and you will live!"*

For all our shortcomings, the church is still the place where God breathes life into our dead bodies and helps us to rise up to become a mighty army -- the church! *"Then you will know that I am God. I will put my Spirit in you, and you will live!"*

Prayer Challenge: Pray for God's renewing spirit.

January 29 – "Hang in There?"

Ephesians 6:10-20

When people come to me for spiritual guidance and counseling, I listen carefully and try to offer sound practical and Biblical advice but at one point I occasionally say; ***"Hang in there!"*** Poor choice of words!

A couple with marital problems: "*Hang in there? What is that supposed to mean?*" An alcoholic struggling with addiction: "*Hang in there? Is he really listening to me?*" A friend diagnosed with cancer: "*Hang in there? Does he think I'm a bat or what?*"

People, desperately looking for hope, instead receive a canned response:" Hang *in there!*" They could watch a talk show for better advice. I sincerely meant what I said, but to someone else it could mean: *"I don't care enough about you to give a meaningful answer, so 'hang in there!'"*

Larry, what do you really mean when you say, *"Hang in there?"* I thought you would never ask. The Bible calls it among other things: **persistence.**

In Romans 2:7 – "He will give eternal life to those who persist in doing what is good." Ephesians 6:10 & 18 – "Be strong with the Lord's mighty power. Put on all of

God's armor so that you will be able to stand firm. Stay alert and be persistent in your prayers for all Christians everywhere." In Matthew 24:13-14 – "But those who endure to the end will be saved. And the Good News about the Kingdom will be preached throughout the whole world."

Persistence and endurance are critical to our faith and to our testimony: *If you persist in doing what is good -- Be strong -- Stay alert -- Be persistent in your prayers -- But those who endure --* God understands your troubles, your disappointments and pain and says: "Be persistent or as I say, 'Hang in there.'"

And if you persist? If you endure? *He gives eternal life -- you will stand firm -- you will be saved -- the Good News will be preached throughout the world --* All part of God's reward for persistence.

Are you having your own struggles? Remember the promises of Scripture: Persist in doing what is good. Be strong. In other words? "Hang in there." God is with you.

Prayer Challenge: Help me to trust God, to be strong and persist.

January 30 – God's Relief for Anxiety

1 Peter 4:7-10

I was feeling anxious and concerned, unable to sleep, I started praying and searching through Scripture and discovered this:

"Be clear minded and self-controlled so that you can pray. Above all, love each other deeply because love covers over a multitude of sins. Offer hospitality to one another without grumbling. Each one should use whatever gift they have received to serve others, faithfully administering God's grace in its various forms." 1 Peter 4:7-10

Are you struggling with anxiety? Feeling the stress? Be clear minded and self-controlled as you pray for God to guide you to more deeply love others, to be hospitable to those around you and to better use your gifts to serve others.

Later, I shared my struggles and what I learned with a group at church. Then I passed out a page filled with Scripture verses. I asked each person to pick a verse and share how that passage relieved anxious feelings.

One woman read from Philippians: "Do not be anxious about anything but in everything by prayer and supplication with thanksgiving let your request be made known to God. And the peace of God, which surpasses all understanding will guard your hearts and your minds in Christ Jesus." (4:6-7) This verse was given to her during a difficult time. Seeing it again offered encouragement that God was continuing to relieve her anxiety.

Another read from 1 Peter: "Casting all your anxieties on God, because God cares for you." (5:7) This brought comfort during a crisis with one of his grandchildren. He knew it by heart and began crying as he shared the meaning with us.

One Scripture after another was read followed by a story of how God relieved anxious moments but more importantly how God worked miracles during their struggles.

Are you feeling anxious? "Trust in the Lord with all your heart and do not lean on your own understanding. In all your ways acknowledge him and he will make straight your paths." (Proverbs 3:5-6) If you acknowledge and trust God, you will find relief.

God taught our group and me a valuable lesson. During anxious moments, trust God to see you through. I pray that during your anxious moments, you discover God's relief.

Prayer Challenge: Help me turn to Scripture for relief from anxiety.

January 31 – Are You the Messiah?

Luke 7:18-23

Keeping up with the news of the day is depressing. On any given day, War, Conflict, Natural Disasters, Financial Crisis, Corruption. Even the commercials are gloomy. One ad after another advocating medicine to restore your health and happiness. But then you hear a long list of side-effects warning of dire consequences or even death if you use the medicine. Sigh!

In the Bible, John the Baptist sent two disciples to Jesus to ask: "Are you the Messiah we've been expecting, or should we keep looking for someone else?"

That's a fair question, isn't it? Life is difficult and full of challenges. We hope you are the Messiah, but we're not sure: "Jesus, are you the Messiah, we long for, pray for and desperately need?" I am also tempted to ask: Jesus, are you the Messiah? Can you provide a ray of hope amidst all our troubles?

Jesus answers: "Tell what you have seen and heard— the blind see, the lame walk, those with leprosy are cured, the deaf hear, the dead are raised to life, and the Good News is being preached to the poor." In other words: Don't let the bad news distract. People are healed, lives are changed, and miracles still occur.

One couple recently described their miracle. "Our son was ten months old and running temps of over 105. Diagnosed with meningitis, he was in the hospital for ten days and we were going nuts until the antibiotics started bringing down the fever. This experience along with last year's cancer scare with our granddaughter clearly highlights two things. 1) God does watch over and comforts us during trying times. 2) God constantly reinforces families with encouragement. "

"'It's going to be alright' has tremendous impact and makes all the difference in the world. That's what we needed to hear. And you know what? It did turn out alright. We are examples of literally hundreds of testimonies and miracles: people healed, lives changed, miracles happening all around us."

Do you remember the original question? "Jesus, are you the Messiah?" I realize now that a good answer is not just 'Yes' but 'Yes' with the knowledge that Jesus has proven and continues to prove He is the Messiah because people are healed, lives are changed, and miracles happen.

Just ask a couple whose infant son was healed. Better yet, share your own story. This week, I encourage you to think about how Jesus has been the Messiah for you. Your story could be just what someone else needs to hear.

Prayer Challenge: How has Jesus been the Messiah for you? Share your story.

February

February 1 – An Audacious Miracle!

2 Kings 6:24 – 7:20

Samaria in Israel was surrounded by the enemy and slowly starving to death. Bird droppings and donkey heads were being sold on the streets for food. Even little children were being fought over by parents to be eaten as food. Humanity had sunk to its lowest possible level. It could not get any worse.

The prophet, Elisha confronted the leaders: "By this time tomorrow, there will be so much food, bushels of flour will be sold for pennies." One leader questioned such a bold prophecy, so Elishah pointed his finger and replied: "You'll see it with your own eyes, but you will never taste any of it!"

What a wild prediction: famine to feast in 24 hours. Donkey head soup to a chicken in every pot! Is this election year politics filled with empty promises? No! This promise is from God. But how? What could God possibly do?

Meanwhile, near the outside wall of the city were four men with leprosy, a gruesome disease. Anyone with leprosy was considered an outcast from society. These poor men could not even remain in the city to starve with the rest of the people. They were shunned, feared, and abandoned.

But one leper had an idea. "Why stay here to die? Let's go to the enemy camps outside the gate and surrender. If they spare us, we might get some food and live. If they kill us, we're dying anyway!" They all agreed, so in the middle of the night, four starving lepers shuffled their way down the hill to the enemy camp to surrender and hopefully get a meal. Here comes the audacious miracle!

The sound of the lepers shuffling was somehow magnified to resemble the attack of a mighty army. The sleeping soldiers heard the noise, panicked, and ran for their lives leaving weapons, clothes, and food behind. What made these hardened soldiers run? The sound of four sick, starving lepers stumbling down the mountain to surrender.

As the lepers reached the camp they were greeted with silence and the inviting aroma of fresh pepperoni pizza. "It's party time!" one shouted. They ate and drank, carried away money, clothes and all the food they could eat.

Then they said to each other: "We're not doing right. This is a day of "Good News" and we are keeping it to ourselves. We must report this to the city." So, the lepers went back to the city.

So... why is this story in the Bible? What are the lessons? Tune in tomorrow!

Prayer Challenge: If God can use four lepers, what can God do through you?

February 2 – An Audacious Miracle – Conclusion

2 Kings 7

The lepers said to each other: "We're not doing right. This is a day of "Good News" and we are keeping it to ourselves. We must report this to the city."

At first the leaders of the city didn't believe the lepers, but they sent a scouting party and found everything to be true. The enemy vanished leaving everything behind. The city gates opened, and everyone rushed out to eat and confiscate whatever could be found. Food was so plentiful that a bushel of flour could now be sold for pennies as predicted.

The leader who originally questioned the prophet was assigned the duty of standing at the front gate and counting everything. But in the confusion, he was trampled to death by the crowd, never tasting any of God's riches, all as the prophet, Elisha, predicted.

Wild? Yes, but true. (Not the pizza) But what can we learn from this strange story?

Tragedy is a part of life: The city, Samaria, suffered just as you and I occasionally suffer. God is always present even when a city is suffering or when we are suffering as represented by the Prophet Elisha: God never abandons us.

The four lepers took an important first step in recognizing the reality of their circumstances. They had the humility and the desperation to ask for help. Then, the lepers took shuffling steps of faith toward change. Those shuffling first steps were miraculously magnified by God to create an audacious miracle.

Ordinary Humans are often used by God to accomplish miracles: Four Lepers? Our bold faith and willingness to take risks honors God. If God can use four lepers to accomplish an audacious miracle, just think what can be done with you and me!

Hearing this remarkable story gave me the courage to give up my business career and take my first tentative, shuffling steps toward ministry. My prayer is that hearing this story inspires you to recognize the reality of where you are and take those shuffling first or second or third steps toward the miracle of God's ever-present help and grace.

Prayer Challenge: What shuffling steps can you take toward better serving God?

February 3 – A Servant

Matthew 20:20-28

There is a once-a-year ritual for United Methodist pastors and leaders called Annual Conference. Several thousand people gather in a civic center for three days of business, worship services and reports. Every moment is scripted, and the keeper of that script is the Conference Director. He or she sits near the Bishop always ready to adjust the script.

One year, a woman worked her way to the Director's table. She was crying and obviously distressed. The Director immediately walked her to a quiet place, and worked out a way to help her. Then as conference was going on all around us, he reached for her hands and began to pray with her.

This extraordinarily busy and pressured church leader dropped everything to help someone in distress. He could have easily handed her off but sensed she would only be satisfied talking to him. This conference director had the heart of a servant, whose love for Jesus ruled.

Christians are called to follow in the footsteps of Jesus Christ. Today we have many churches and denominations offering different teachings, all claiming they are following the right path of Jesus. Which ones are right? My hunch is that all of us are mostly right and all of us could do better.

But, when it comes to following Jesus, love must rule our hearts. To love is first a choice, then it grows into a commitment filled with joys and problems. At times love becomes a crucial responsibility but when the love of Christ truly leads and guides our lives, we become more unified than divided, filled with a faith that is stronger than our doubts.

This is a critical lesson. Our testimony as Christians, as followers of Jesus is wrapped up in our willingness to express our love by taking on the role of servant in everything we do. Acts of caring as you take on the role of servant is the best way to show others how love rules your heart.

The Conference Director demonstrated the heart of a servant guided by the example of Jesus. There is nothing easy or glamorous about being a servant, but the reward is heavenly. Who can you be a servant for today?

Prayer Challenge: Help me be a servant for someone today.

February 4 – Persistent Prayer

Luke 18:1-8

We pray about something important or painful. We hope for a response of comfort and understanding but no answer comes. We then ask: "Where is God? Does God care about me?" In the movie, "Oh God, Book II," a little girl asks George Burns aka God: "Why do bad things happen to us?"

George Burns answers: "That's the way the system works. Have you ever seen an up, without a down? A front, without a back? A top without a bottom? You can't have one without the other. I discovered that if I take away sad, then I take away happy, too. They go together." Then with a smile he adds, "If somebody has a better idea. I hope they put it in the suggestion box."

Prayer, persistent prayer, continual prayer, a habit of prayer even when God seems to be quiet is an important part of strengthening our relationship with God. Scripture confirms the importance of persistence:

- Ephesians 6:18 – Pray in the Spirit at all times and on every occasion. Stay alert and be persistent in your prayers for all believers everywhere.
- James 5:16 – The earnest prayer of a righteous person has great power and produces wonderful results.

- 1 Thessalonians 5:17 – Never stop praying.
- Romans 8:26 – We don't know what God wants us to pray for. But the Holy Spirit prays for us with groanings that cannot be expressed in words.
- Romans 12:12 – Rejoice in our confident hope. Be patient in trouble and keep on praying.

Prayer should be described as the steering wheel on a car guiding us where we need to go. Unfortunately for many of us, prayer is more like the spare tire, seldom used or needed until something goes flat.

When we pray and God seems quiet, we continue to pray and trust God is listening. One pastor wrote: "We sometimes look to God to answer our prayers as if He were the waiter who takes our order and swiftly returns with steaming plates of what we ask for. That is not God's way. He hears our prayers and responds but in God's way, in God's time. Can we trust and accept?"

Persistent prayer is about trusting God to lead and guide us. We seek a deeper relationship. We cling to faith through obstacles and discouragement. God hears our prayers. We are not forgotten. So, through it all, we continue to pray, trusting that God listens and responds in God's way, in God's time.

Prayer Challenge: Work on a habit of daily prayer. Stick to it for 30 Days.

February 5 – Riding a Dead Horse

Matthew 16:13-26

Bill Dettmer wrote: "The tribal wisdom of the Dakota Indians, passed on from one generation to the next, says that when you discover you are riding a dead horse, the best strategy is to dismount. However, in modern times, because of an unwillingness to let things go, we often try other strategies, such as:"

Buy a stronger whip. Change riders. Threaten the horse with termination. Appoint a committee to study the horse. Lower the standard so that dead horses can be included. Reclassifying the dead horse as living impaired. Harnessing several dead horses together for increased speed. Donate the dead horse to a recognized charity. Time management study to see if lighter rides would improve productivity. Promote the dead horse to a supervisory position.

I laughed so hard typing this, tears were clouding my vision. But within the humor there is a grain of truth. Over the years, I imagine we've all seen a few dead horses in our lives or our careers, our families and even in our churches.

Matthew 28:19-20 – Jesus says: "Go and make disciples of all nations, baptizing them in the name of the Father and of the Son and the Holy Spirit and teach them to obey everything I have taught you."

Our mission? Reach out to others as potential disciples, offer solid teaching and pass on the comfort and hope of knowing Jesus Christ as Lord and Savior.

So, if our main goal as a church is to reach out to others in the name of Christ, then we need to be more aware of how people communicate. Sunday services inside the comfort of church buildings has less impact on a world dominated by cell phones and social media. How can our church more effectively communicate Christ's mission to make and teach disciples?

And to each of us? How well do you know the people who live next door, across the street or behind you? Do you know the names of their children? How are they doing? How can you be a better neighbor? Ask: "How can I pray for you?"

Two important questions: How can I as a Christian make a difference in the lives of those I meet? How can I be part of a church that continually does the same?

Do we have the courage to dismount from the dead horses that slow us down and concentrate on the challenges ahead? It's not easy but serving God was never meant to be easy. God never said, "Get up on that dead horse and ride." Jesus said: "Take up your cross and follow me."

Prayer Challenge: What dead horses stand between you and serving God?

February 6 – Storms & John Wesley

Romans Chapter 3

While exploring St. Simons Island, Georgia, I discovered roadside plaques recognizing the contributions of John and Charles Wesley, founders of the United Methodist Church. Curious to know more, I visited a bookstore to see what local historians had to say about the brothers and their only visit to America.

In 1736, John and Charles, arrived from England to St. Simons Island to oversee the church and fulfill their dream of witnessing to Native Americans. According to local historians the trip was a failure. They were not prepared for the harsh living conditions. John wearing formal attire even in the woods and holding worship services as if he were in London seemed odd. People mostly laughed at him.

John fell in love but couldn't make up his mind whether to marry. He should have, but he didn't. Tired of waiting, his sweetheart married someone else. Furious, John refused to serve communion to the newly married couple. This unfortunate incident turned out to be the last straw. John found himself back on a ship headed toward England. Charles left months earlier.

So, by all accounts the Wesley brothers' trip to Georgia was a failure. So why would St. Simons, honor them?

Part of the answer occurred during a ferocious storm on the ship returning to England. John, depressed because of his failed mission, was heartbroken, seasick, and scared out of his wits. Yet, it was at this point that John's life took a dramatic change.

While on deck, holding desperately to anything solid, John noticed several families near the stern serenely singing hymns. He couldn't believe it! How could they conduct worship and sing in the midst of such a terrible storm? Why weren't they more frightened? John marveled at their faith and vowed to learn more. Weeks after arriving home, John continued contemplating his unhappiness in contrast to the people contentedly singing.

Then, John heard someone reading from a commentary on Romans: "Since we have been made right in God's sight by faith, we have peace with God." These words beautifully described God's amazing grace. (Romans 3:28)

John would later write: "I felt my heart strangely warmed." What warmed his heart was the realization that faith was not earned by hard work. Rather, faith comes from the heart and from a strengthened relationship with God through Jesus Christ. We think religious satisfaction only comes from doing. John learned that faith comes not from 'doing' something but from 'being' something.

Next: More on John Wesley, Storms and Faith.

February 7 – John Wesley and Faith

Romans Chapter 8

John Wesley wrote: "I felt my heart strangely warmed." Faith comes from the heart and from a strengthened relationship with God through Jesus Christ. We think religious satisfaction only comes from doing. John learned that faith comes not from 'doing' something but from 'being' something. Our shortcomings overcome by God's mercy and forgiveness. Our flaws overcome by God's grace. Our sins overcome by God's love.

Faith is not as much about us and what we do as it is about God's gift appreciating the awesomeness of God's grace. Faith is about living our lives based on sharing that same precious gift we received with others.

A changed John Wesley began preaching but this time the passion was evident as he spoke of faith and God's grace. Local preachers, feeling uncomfortable with John's enthusiasm, refused to invite him back. But it no longer mattered, for John was preaching throughout the countryside. John began preaching so often that groups or societies began to form. Others tried to stop the movement but, the more they tried to stop him, the more popular he became.

John formed small groups or societies based on personal accountability, discipleship, and teaching. These societies would become the foundation for Methodist churches all over the world. Charles Wesley provided music, and wrote lyrics for more than 6,000 hymns, including, "Hark, the Herald Angels Sing."

Near the end of his life, no one in all of England — including the king — was more recognizable than John Wesley. He would get up at four in the morning, preach at five and by six was back in the saddle. John delivered more than 42,000 sermons, an average of 15 per week and rode between sixty and seventy miles a day. He did this until well into his eighties.

Today, John Wesley is remembered for:
- Evangelism – "The world is my parish." He said it over and over. "I didn't wait for people to come to me. I went out to find them."
- Organization – "Good organization helps the fruits of evangelism be conserved and expanded." He organized the people called Methodist.
- Education – He believed in teaching and learning and was a prolific writer. The printed page was as important to him as preaching.

Sometimes, it's the storms that teach the ultimate lessons. Visit Saint Simons, Georgia or any United Methodist church to see God's gift of grace in action.

Prayer Challenge: Read Romans 12 and pray how God impacts you.

February 8 – A Bear & Running Shoes

Luke 9:23-27

An older man was hiking in the woods with a young friend when they stumbled upon an angry bear. Both men took off running but it was obvious that the bear was going to overtake them if something didn't happen soon. The older man stopped, quickly pulled off his boots and began to slip on running shoes.

"You can't outrun a bear, even in those shoes!" the younger man cried out.

The older man said: *"I don't have to outrun that bear. **I only have to outrun you!"***

This says a lot about our world. Selfishness and greed are celebrated, and allegiance and loyalty undermined. In business, "job security" is replaced with "corporate downsizing" and "company loyalty" becomes "upward mobility."

"I don't have to outrun the bear. I only have to outrun you!"

That phrase may define our culture, but it does not have to define you and I. We choose to be different. Jesus offers the bread of life so we will never be hungry again. Jesus establishes the example of unselfish, sacrificial love. If we have faith in Christ, we show the same unselfish sacrificial love. The secret is our faith in Christ.

People ask me: Why do I need to go to church? I can be bored anywhere. Why dress up and go there?

My answer? If you are going to be a Christian, you've signed on to the most fulfilling adventure of all time and you are going to need all the encouragement and support you can get. That's what the church should be doing best. Providing the support to carry out your mission.

Here is another possible ending to that story. The older man stops to put on his running shoes and hands another pair to his partner. "Put these on and run with me," he says. "Together, with God's help, we can both outrun the bear."

That is the Spirit of Christ at work: Running Shoes for two. Guided and motivated by the life-giving love of Jesus Christ.

Prayer Challenge: Who is encouraging and supporting you in your faith walk?

February 9 – $7.43

James 2:14-17

The checkout lines at the grocery store were long and I was in a hurry. Seeing one line nearly empty, I slipped over and stood behind a young twenty-something woman with a cart containing ten to twelve jars of baby food. Nothing else; just baby food.

"This is great," I thought. "She'll only be a minute and I can be on my way."

The clerk took the woman's check for seven dollars and forty-three cents and slid it into the proper slot on the cash register. At this point the drawer was supposed to open while a receipt was printed, but not this time. A light began to blink: "See Manager." The clerk called on the intercom for the supervisor while running the check through again on her register. The same sign flashing: "See Manager."

"Oh no!" I thought. "Not another delay."

The supervisor arrived and without looking at the register, picked up the check and began to quietly talk to the customer while easing her toward the door. Her check for seven dollars and forty-three cents was no good and the manager was quietly saying she could not buy her baby food. The clerk set her groceries aside and began to ring up my purchase.

Jesus teaches: "You are the light of the world. We don't light a lamp and put it under a bowl. Instead, we put it on a stand, and it gives light to everyone in the house. In the same way, let your light shine so they may see your good deeds and praise your Father in heaven." (Mat. 5:14-16)

Every day, you and I receive opportunities to help someone. Our light shines when we use those God-given opportunities to witness our faith by getting involved. There is nothing dramatic about these day-to-day encounters, but they emphatically tell the world what kind of Christians we really are.

At this point, I want to finish the story by writing how I approached the manager and offered to pay for the purchase of the baby food. It was the right thing to do. I didn't have much money, but I could afford seven dollars and forty-three cents. Instead, hiding my light under a bowl, I turned my head and walked away. There are no acceptable excuses. I had an opportunity to help someone and failed.

What we believe as Christians only works if we turn our faith into action. How about you? How many opportunities have you missed to let your light shine and instead hid it under a bowl?

Prayer Challenge: Be alert for God-given opportunities to let your light shine.

February 10 – $7.43 Lives On

1 Peter 4:10-11

A few years ago, I visited Tom Riddle, a former boss and friend, to talk about my first book and share old stories. But instead of small talk, Tom taught a unique lesson on giving. At one point, he said: "I read your book and loved your story on "$7.43." Tom looked at me, smiled and said: "What have you done since then?"

"Well, I've helped a few people." I stammered weakly.

"I've got an idea," he said and picked up the phone and instructed his office manager to bring him a check for $743.00 and said: "I want you to take this money and put it into envelopes and give it to 100 people in need." Then, Mr. Riddle said: "This is my gift and I'm happy to do it. Now, what will you do?"

What could I say? Mr. Riddle had given something of value, and it was my turn to respond. But how could a preacher give a gift that would make a difference?

Peter wrote: "Each one should use whatever gift they have received to serve others, faithfully administering God's grace in its various forms." The message is that all of us have something to give of great value. We need to find it and use it.

A soft voice inside me kept saying: "The best gift you can give is your new book."

"But Lord," I weakly replied: "I haven't even paid the printing bill yet!" Several days later at a community gathering, I shared the story of Mr. Riddle's gift and passed out 50 envelopes each with $7.43 along with fifty copies of my book. On Sunday, fifty people in our church were given the same opportunity.

Mr. Riddle visited our church later and heard the stories:

- One woman experiencing divorce took the kids out to eat and read the book.
- Another gift was sent to a man in prison who used the money for his daughter's Christmas and passed the book around to fellow inmates.
- A third gift was given to a family struggling through a recent job layoff.

One person after another told a story of a gift given and how they became more involved. They spoke of the joy of offering something encouraging to a person in need. We were given the opportunity to participate in a miracle.

Mr. Riddle taught a valuable lesson on the importance and joy of giving: All for $7.43. The lesson of $7.43 means God is calling us to be alert for opportunities to make a difference in the community around us. How will you respond?

Prayer Challenge: How can you use your gifts and talents to help someone else?

February 11 – "The Impossible Dream"

Jeremiah 29:11-13

"Impossible Dream" is my favorite song within "Man of La Mancha." The story is based on "Don Quixote," by Cervantes about an old man who reads books on knights and chivalry. He self-proclaims himself a knight, Don Quixote de La Mancha and rides off pursuing noble quests with his faithful squire, Sancho.

They spot a windmill and mistake it for a four-armed giant and a rundown inn for a castle. Within that inn/castle, Quixote meets Aldonza, a woman who has seen hard times. Quixote changes Aldonza's name to Dulcinea meaning, "sweetness of a tender lover." For Quixote, Dulcinea is a princess with whom he pledges to defend her honor.

An old man with visions of impossible dreams pledging his undying love to a woman who once had big dreams but settled for much less. Two depressing answers to the question: "What happens to our big dreams?" For many of us, big dreams were compromised by the oftentimes harsh reality of daily living.

Microbiologists end up delivering mail. Pastors sell stocks and bonds. Geniuses end up behind bars. But our dreams do not have to die. Big dreams may be put aside or altered but giving them up was never God's plan. "'For I know the plans I have for you,' says the LORD. 'They are plans for good and not for disaster, to give you a future and a hope.'" (Jeremiah 29:11-12) God has plans for you. When you pray, God will listen and if you look for God in earnest, you will find Him.

Near the end of the play, Don Quixote is lying in bed near death, dreams shattered. Sancho tries to cheer him up, but the old man says his knightly quest was just a dream. Aldonza forces her way into the old man's bedroom because she can no longer bear to be anyone but Dulcinea. When he does not recognize her, she helps him remember.

She says, "Once you found a girl and called her Dulcinea. When you spoke the name, an angel seemed to whisper, Dulcinea. Won't you bring back the dream of Dulcinea?"

The old man whispers, "Perhaps it was not a dream."

Next: A new ending to "Man of La Manch and "The Impossible Dream."

February 12 – "The Impossible Dream" Lives On

Proverbs 3:5-8

Dulcinea says to Quixote, "You spoke of a dream. And about the quest. How you must fight, and it doesn't matter whether you win or lose if only you follow the quest."

He rises from the bed: "The words! Tell me the words!

She continues: "To dream the impossible dream. To fight the unbeatable foe. To bear with unbearable sorrow. To run where the brave dare not go."

Suddenly, the old man rises from his bed, calling for his armor and sword so that he may set out again, but it is too late. He cries out and falls dead. Sancho is distraught but Aldonza says, "the old man may be dead, but Don Quixote de La Mancha lives on."

The dream has been planted in Aldonza. The Impossible Dream is alive. Do you ever wonder what happened next? Well, I discovered a never-before-seen script that follows the original play. Would you like to hear what happened next? Of course you would!

Aldonza becomes Dulcinea and continues to work at the inn, but she never forgets the Impossible Dream.

The owner retires and helps Dulcinea purchase the old rundown inn. She immediately makes improvements and takes over the cooking.

Her inn is renamed "Dulcinea Castle" and soon develops a reputation for serving the finest food and providing excellent service. With the profits from Dulcinea Castle along with the approval and financial help from the priest and local church, she opens a school offering quality education for boys and girls with equal opportunities for all. The school is aptly named "The Don Quixote School of Impossible Dreams."

"This is my quest, to follow that star. No matter how hopeless, no matter how far. To fight for the right, without question or pause. To be willing to march into hell for a heavenly cause. And I know if I'll only be true, to this glorious quest, that my heart will lie peaceful and calm when I'm laid to my rest. And the world will be better for this. And one man, sore and covered with scars, still strove with their last ounce of courage to reach the unreachable, the unreachable... star."

Prayer Challenge: What is your "Impossible Dream?" How is God involved?

February 13 – Humble Pie

Luke 14 :1-24

Flannery O'Connor wrote about Mrs. Turpin, so sure of her heavenly destination until the end of the story when she has a vision where she sees a crowd of souls moving toward heaven. To her shock, at the head of the line is a group of criminals, followed by poor folks. At the end, she sees her group. Their feelings of superiority and outward goodness is stripped away. Only the grace of God allows them to enter heaven along with the rest.

Mrs. Turpin has the right attributes of a church-going Christian, yet she is surprised to see herself in the back of the line going to heaven. Jesus says, "The door to heaven is narrow. Work hard to get in but many will try and fail." What happened to grace? Grace is there but what will you do with it?

We have the freedom to choose our destiny, however there are consequences. The wide gate is easier with a life free of spiritual responsibilities. Believe anything. Do anything. The narrow door seems more restrictive at first. Some freedoms might be sacrificed but those sacrifices count for something.

Jesus then says: "For those who exalt themselves will be humbled, and those who humble themselves will be exalted." Could humility be at the heart of what Jesus is teaching about the narrow door? Yes, but the answer is not to strive to become one of the humblest persons in the world." And tomorrow you do really well, take a selfie and post it on Facebook.

There is a cardboard sign outside a children's clubhouse stating the rules for belonging: 1. Nobody act big. 2. Nobody act small. 3. Everybody act medium.

A devotion mentioned an ad for a company that will deliver and throw a pie in the face of anyone chosen. Crazy? Picture this: A well-tailored and arrogant preacher comes to the door. A delivery person is there with a special package. Is it a gift? The delivery person with a big smile on his face, opens the box. Before the preacher can say, "Hallelujah," he whips a pie out of the box and, "Smash!"

The lesson? A pie in the face brings a person's dignity down to where it should be and puts the big people on the same level as everyone else.

Remember the rules: Nobody act big. Nobody act small. Everybody act medium. Good advice from a clubhouse of kids. We need to follow that advice before someone decides we need a pie in the face.

Prayer Challenge: How can we pursue the narrow door with humility?

February 14 – Love and Weddings

1 Corinthians chapter 13

I have officiated literally hundreds of weddings over the years, each one beautiful in its own way. There was a wedding for my nephew. They wanted a service on a beach within a few miles of their home. The beach was a special part of their lives so it seemed only natural for the bride and groom to say their vows before God and guests in the midst of the surf and sand.

The Apostle Paul understood how important it was to truly love one another. The thirteenth chapter of First Corinthians over the years has become the favorite for couples making the lifelong commitment to love each other before God.

"If I could speak all the languages of earth and of angels, but didn't love others, I would only be a noisy gong or a clanging cymbal. If I had the gift of prophecy, and if I understood all of God's plans and possessed all knowledge, and if I had such faith I could move mountains, but didn't love others, I would be nothing. If I gave everything I have to the poor and sacrificed my body, I could boast about it; but if I didn't love others, I would have gained nothing." (1 Corinthians 13:1-3))

One wedding was held on a nearby farm. We were welcomed and given an old-fashioned hand fan with the service printed on the fan. The wedding took place directly in front of the barn. Above the couple was a sign: "This is Where Our Story Begins…"

"Love is patient and kind. Love is not jealous or boastful or proud or rude. It does not demand its own way. It is not irritable, and it keeps no record of being wronged. It does not rejoice about injustice but rejoices whenever the truth wins out. Love never gives up, never loses faith, is always hopeful, and endures through every circumstance." (4-7)

During the wedding service, the bride and groom answered the traditional vows but then added words of their own. Both told of their undying love for each other and how they would help each other no matter what. The couple chose to express their love for God and each other by planting a seed. Dirt was provided by each of the parents. Then the bride and groom carefully planted the seeds together. Then the pastor talked of God being a vital part of the relationship as he poured water over the freshly planted soil.

"Three things last—faith, hope, and love—and the greatest is love." Weddings symbolize the love of a couple as they stand before God and express their vows to have and to hold, from this day forward, for better for worse, for richer for poorer, in sickness and in health, to love and to cherish, until parted by death.

Prayer Challenge: Read 1 Corinthians 13 and pray how God can guide your love.

February 15 – "Free, Free, Free"

Luke 12:32-34, Luke 18:18-30

Mell and I moved from a house full of furniture and stuff to a small condominium. So, in addition to the normal stress and strain of moving we also faced a serious dilemma. How do we reduce our possessions by more than 50%? How do you eliminate half of everything you own? Jesus said: "Sell your possessions and give to those in need. This will store up treasure for you in heaven!" (Luke 12:33)

Mell and I faced a dilemma. We could sell everything, or we could give it away. Although the decision was painful at first, we chose to give everything away.

Each day, I filled up a truck or my car and took everything to a Community Mission. Throughout the building, we placed mementos, dishes, furniture, tools, lawn equipment, books and pictures. The sign simply said, "Free."

As word circulated, people would gather. At times they would linger picking up something, then put it down. Some would ask, "Are you serious? Is this free?" One lady said, "I can give this to my sister." Another smiled and said, "Thank you." One person saw the sign, "Free," and picked up the bookcase holding many of the items and started to walk out. We had to stop him.

For several days, the building was like a shopping mall, filled with interesting stuff. Looking back on the experience I learned some significant lessons:

1. **Pain turns to joy.** The decision to part with your stuff is painful but at some part of the process, giving generously and creatively becomes a joy.
2. **Possessions can possess you.** The more you have, the more you care for and protect. Letting possessions go can be a liberating experience.
3. **Stuff is stuff.** Material things provide little lasting value, but kindness and generosity have the potential to change lives and witness your faith.

Jesus told a rich man: "Sell your possessions and give the money to the poor, and you will have treasure in heaven." (Luke 18:22) I am not rich but over the years, I accumulated a lot of stuff. Parting with it was hard but the pain was soon replaced by a feeling of satisfaction and joy more valuable.

Jesus says: "I assure you that everyone who has given up house or wife or brothers or parents or children, for the sake of the Kingdom of God, will be repaid many times over in this life, and will have eternal life." -- Luke 18: 29-30

Prayer Challenge: What can you give away for something more valuable?

February 16 – Awareness

Luke 16:19-31

Patrick Lencioni asks six questions for any organization seeking purpose. Why do we exist? How do we behave? What do we do? How will we succeed? What is most important right now? Who must do what? Lencioni writes: "Answering these questions is as difficult as it is simple. Simple because it doesn't require great intellectual capacity or cleverness. Difficult because it requires honest dialogue and real commitment."

Jesus' story in Luke seems to be about money. But dig deeper and you find a connection with Lencioni's six questions. This story is more about awareness. The rich man in the story was chomping on Kentucky Fried Chicken and passing by starving Lazarus, completely unaware of what's going on.

God is not condemning us for being healthy or wealthy or talented or highly educated or successful. God is warning us to be more aware and more vigilant about using our health, our wealth, our talents, our education, and our success to benefit others in service of Jesus Christ.

We go back to Lencioni's six simple questions. Our church group recently asked the questions and began looking for ways to respond to local needs. We found: In addition to paying for food, rent, and utilities people struggle with old vehicles needing repairs. We responded by setting up a voucher system for local car repair shops to cover the cost of repairs for those who needed help. By taking the time to pray and ask about local needs, we were able to provide practical help.

"God won't ask what kind of car you drove, but he'll ask how many people you offered a ride. God won't ask how many clothes are in your closet, but he'll ask how many you helped clothe. God won't ask about your social status; He will ask what kind of class you displayed to others. God won't ask about your material possessions, but he'll ask if they dictated your life. God won't ask about your salary, but he will ask if you compromised your character to get it." (Unknown)

Why do we exist? How do we behave? What do we do? How will we succeed? What is most important right now? Who must do what? May we use these questions as part of our prayer and devotion time to enable us to become more aware of the needs around us. May God guide us to creatively respond.

Prayer Challenge: This week read Luke 16:19-31 and answer the six questions.

February 17 – "It's Your Church. It's God's Church"

Luke 18:9-17

Mike Abrashoff wrote "It's Your Ship." Upon taking command of the USS Benfold he saw the opportunity to do something different. He called it the Golden Rule approach. Mike put himself in his sailors' shoes and interviewed every sailor on the ship to find out what they valued and then made changes. He sent cooks to culinary school, offered college courses and asked officers to treat sailors with respect. He empowered everyone to make decisions and work to make their ship the best in the Navy, encouraging them with the words, "It's your ship."

What a great way to describe the ideal church. "It's not my church. It's your church. It's God's church." God empowers us to look around and work to make our church the best we can be. Easier said than done.

A pastor wrote: "One problem people have is the closer they come to God, the more clearly they see weaknesses in others. The temptation is to be critical of those who do not share your ideals. The secret to Christian life however is to hate the wrong, yet still feel love and tolerance for the one who does wrong. The problem does not grow less as we grow as Christians, the problem increases."

When we first become Christians, we often go through a period of repentance. We recognize our faults and sins and ask for God's forgiveness. Then we make changes in our life to please God. But as we do that, we also see more clearly the faults and sins of others, and we feel the need to do something about it. "We straightened up our lives so why can't everyone else straighten out as well?"

Comparing our lives with others may enable us to look pretty good, but God wants us to look up and when we compare our life with God, we come up short.

This is a warning to keep our eyes focused on God, not others. Comparing yourself to God will always keep you humble. The second lesson is about hope. No matter who you are, there is always God's promise of forgiveness and complete acceptance. Jesus said, "For those who exalt themselves will be humbled, and those who humble themselves will be exalted." – Luke 18:14

It's not my church. It's your church. It's God's church. The challenge is for each of us to look around with genuine humility and figure out how we can more effectively practice one word: encouragement.

Mike Abrashoff wrote: "Good began to happen when he went for the golden rule. I put people first, and as a result I was paid a thousand times over."

Prayer Challenge: Ask God to help you encourage someone today?

February 18 – The Church: Judgment

Hebrews 10:23-25

Our family moved to a new area just as I entered the seventh grade. During the first week of school, I tried out for the chorus. Since, I grew up singing in church choirs, school chorus seemed like a great way to start the school year and make a few friends.

The teacher handed me a piece of unfamiliar music and asked me to sing. Based on the looks and snickers of the other children in the room, I was not doing well. Halfway through the song, the teacher stopped playing and said: *"I'm sorry. You are not qualified to sing in our school chorus."*

I remember timidly walking out of the room, embarrassed and devastated, but I recovered from the initial hurt quickly enough and went on to other interests. However, I soon quit the church choir and when singing during worship, began to lower my voice so no one would hear me. Eventually, I asked: "why attend church at all?" I volunteered to work more on Sundays. Then, I simply stopped attending.

Looking back, I realize there were many poor choices made on my part. But -- at any time someone could have stepped in and offered encouragement. Someone at church could have and should have asked: "Why wasn't I singing with the choir or attending youth? Why was I working on Sundays?" They could have checked up on me, but most didn't, so I quietly slipped away.

Does this sound familiar?

There are many reasons people no longer attend church. But for many who choose to stop going to church, something likely happened. While reading this were you reminded of a time when someone said something that hurt you deeply? Maybe there was an occasion when you needed God and/or your church and for whatever reason, you were deeply disappointed.

If you are in the group that left the church or if you've ever been disappointed or hurt by your church or if you just simply want to help your church do better, read tomorrow's devotion. This story has a happy ending.

Prayer Challenge: Has someone, somewhere hurt you deeply? Give it to God.

February 19 – The Church: Encouragement

Hebrews 10:23-25

Shortly after finishing college, I began selling automobiles. Another salesman talked me into visiting church. He said, "It would be good for business." While this is not usually a good reason to attend, I was willing to try. So, one Sunday morning, I showed up at a nearby church and took a seat in the back of the sanctuary. Just then, two men I recognized walked in.

This was trouble. Both men purchased used cars from me. Both had problems and left the dealership dissatisfied. I remember wishing the floor would open and swallow me whole? I tried to scrunch my body behind the pew so they wouldn't see me, but to no avail. They recognized me immediately and walked my way.

"Larry Davies, you've got a lot of nerve showing your face here."

No! That's not what they said, but it is what I expected and probably deserved. Instead? "Larry, what a wonderful surprise."

They offered no judgment. They sat beside me and talked as if we had been friends for years. Two people who should have been angry, reached out the hand of friendship.

Looking back, I realize this was a key moment in my life and I will always be grateful for their encouragement.

Hebrews spoke of encouragement: "Let us think of ways to motivate one another to acts of love and good works. And let us not neglect our meeting together, as some people do, but encourage one another." (Hebrews 10:23-25)

The key is in understanding and utilizing the power of one word: encouragement. Becoming an encourager doesn't simply mean speaking in flowery platitudes but rather looking to motivate others to acts of love and good works.

One Sunday after worship, the choir director walked up and asked: "I heard you singing during worship today and really liked the sound of your voice. Would you be interested in joining our choir?" Thanks to her continuing encouragement, I did join the choir and rediscovered that I could sing – well, sort of. Encouragement works.

God lovingly gives us the freedom to choose how we interact with others. My prayer is that we will all strive to be encouragers who inspire others to outbursts of love and good deeds. Is this what being the church is all about?

We could certainly do worse! Hey, maybe I should sing a solo? Not!!

Prayer Challenge: Help me be on the lookout for new ways to encourage others.

February 20 – Sam
(Letter by Samantha Mingin)

1 John 5:1-5

I asked for stories of how God or our church impacted their lives. Sam sent a letter that says so much about what a church should and could be.

"When you asked the question: "What the church means to me?' I had no idea where to begin. Where do you start and how do you put into words that your life has been forever changed within the last two years of being within these walls?"

"My mom and stepdad started taking me to church when I was in diapers. I grew up in this church and made great friends. I was involved in Vacation Bible School, youth group. You name it; I was part of it. Little did I know my parents and this church were creating in me a foundation of faith."

"During my early adult years, I discovered a passion for leading worship at another church, however, a divorce and becoming a single parent to a 6-month-old led to me being told I was no longer welcome to be the face of worship. I did not turn my back on God, but I did wonder where I was supposed to be."

"I received a call inviting me to join the worship team at my home church. I wasn't sure how I'd make it work but the church welcomed me and my daughter back with open arms. It felt like I was starting to find my place and it brought me so much joy to use my gift to help others experience God's love through music."

"Then came the invite to join a small group. Not going to lie, I put it off for a year. If you're still reading this, take my advice and don't wait as long as I did. I joined a group of people each Sunday and quickly realized they had taken my daughter and I in as one of their own. We became family. God's timing is so, so good."

"Right after joining the group, I became a full-time single parent. This group not only walked alongside us, but they also walked ahead of us; foreseeing challenges and making sure we would never be alone. I realize that I have a village of twelve beautiful souls who will forever be walking through life with me."

Max Lucado writes: "At some point in life, God's love must move from being a concept we wonder about to a conscious experience that transforms us. God's love deserves better than a half-hearted acknowledgement!"

What the church does best will never make headlines. There is no news in a day-to-day habit of loving others the way God loves us. But there is a large population outside and inside our door that needs to see, feel, hear, taste and smell that love. They need what Sam experienced and what God's church is ready to give.

Prayer Challenge: What does or should God's church mean to you?

February 21 – God & Money

Matthew 5:13-16 & Luke 16:1-13

Christians are not immune to financial problems.
The percentage of Christians declaring bankruptcy is
roughly the same as non-Christians. Yet, in Matthew
5, Jesus calls us to be salt and light to the world to
be an example which includes handling resources. I
can't imagine a better testimony than Christians and
churches who practice generosity toward others.

Money has a dark and a light side. The dark is greed
and poor management leading to excessive debt
or extensive hoarding. Churches are not immune.
Sometimes the biggest arguments and disagreements
come when churches are deciding how to spend
a surplus. The light is exercising self-discipline and
generosity. Missions succeed because of giving
individuals and churches.

The parable of the dishonest servant in Luke 16
provides a lesson about our witness and our money.
This Scripture is for those who made the commitment
to follow Jesus and ask: "Now What?" The dishonest
manager was paid to handle the owner's money. In
those days, you collected a certain amount for the
owner and kept the rest, like a commission. But this
manager was greedy and collected too much. The
owner found out and fired him.

So, what the manager did was call in the people who owed money and eliminated his commission. The owner was grateful because he got his money. The manager was grateful because he kept his job. The debtors were grateful because they got a better deal. Shrewd. Very Shrewd.

Question: How can our churches better use financial resources to serve God rather than allow those resources to control us?

A church bought an abandoned block of business property to develop. Within each building, they opened a business within half the property and a ministry with the other half. A restaurant on one side and a food pantry on the other. A warehouse on one end and a youth indoor playground on the other.

Another church manages Potter's House serving the homeless. Beside Potter's House is a Pizza Restaurant that pays rent to the church which is then used to support Potter's House. Shrewd. Very Shrewd. I think Jesus would approve.

Prayer Challenge: How can you be more shrewd in the use of your resources?

February 22 – Stuck in the Mud!

Matthew 6:5-13

What if, God said to you, "Come away with Me for a while. The world, with its nonstop demands, can be put on hold. You live among people who glorify busyness; they made money & time a tyrant that controls their lives. They bought into the illusion that more is better: more money, meetings, programs, activity."

I read this from Sarah Young's "Jesus Calling" during a leadership retreat where we were asking, "Are we doing too much busy work and not enough faith work?" If you want to be around a bunch of Type A, ultra busy, super organized, high-octane people, hang around this group.

Too much "work at it" and not enough "faith in it" is like your car getting stuck in the mud. You push on the accelerator, the roar of the engine, the mud flying in all directions and the smoke rising are signs of frantic activity but the object of all the activity, your car, still sits there stuck in the mud.

Or... you could stop the frantic activity and step out of the car. After looking at the situation more calmly, you realize the need to do something different. You place a board in front of a wheel. This allows your tire to gain needed traction. As you get back in the car, you push the accelerator again but slowly easing the car forward, then backward allowing the car to grip the board and free itself.

Are you spinning wheels, throwing up mud and smoke but going nowhere? Maybe it's time to stop, step away and make time for the God who created you, has a plan for you and is looking for an opportunity to guide and encourage you.

Sarah Young then writes: "Moreover as you walk close to Me, I can bless others through you." So, not only will you benefit from spending time with God but those who watch you, depend upon you, lean on you, love you or even despise you will be blessed by your willingness to listen and follow God's guidance.

I learned busyness is good but not at the expense of missing God's voice and becoming more aware of others. Reciting this simple prayer from "Godspell" is one way to refocus: "Day by day. Dear Lord, three things I pray. To see thee more clearly. Love thee more dearly. Follow thee more nearly. Day by day."

Prayer Challenge: Help me to slow down and make time for You.

February 23 – Tap, Tap, Tap: Worship

Psalm 100

Tap-tap, tap-tap-tap: annoying sounds? Maybe, but it could mean much more. Captain Eugene 'Red' McDaniel tapped on the walls of his cell in the Vietnamese Prisoner of War camp known as the Hanoi Hilton. The taping was a secret code prisoners used to communicate with each other. The number one rule was: "No communication with other prisoners." Anyone caught would be executed.

Isolation was the prime weapon of the communist captors. As the hours slowly turned into days and weeks, Captain McDaniel came to fear the loneliness and the silence far more than any threats of physical harm. The highlight of each day was being taken to the washroom where they told him about the camp code, a series of taps to spell out letters. McDaniel in his book, "Scars and Stripes" came to recognize the code as his lifeline and only link with sanity.

If a new prisoner couldn't learn the code and communicate with fellow prisoners, he would gradually begin to draw inward and deteriorate. As the days dragged on, a prisoner would slowly lose any will to live.

What do codes and POW's have to do with worship? One word: communication. Worship represents our opportunity to communicate with God. More than a hymn, sermon and prayer, worship is the code that becomes our lifeline.

We don't always feel that way. I hear: "I don't get anything out of worship." Followed by a complaint about the pastor or the music. But worship should be a possible turning point not something to endure. Worship is a human response to a divine revelation. Tap-tap: through the quietness of prayer. Tap-tap-tap: through singing a song. Tap-tap-tap-tap: through the prophetic words of a sermon. Worship is the camp code for vital communication with God.

One church was concerned about improving worship. So, a few of the members gathered along with the pastor and spent several evenings discussing the purpose of worship. They studied Scripture, prayed, read a chapter from a book on worship and concluded that worship was "for the love of God." Then they all prayed how they would each make difference for the love of God.

For the love of God... One volunteered to place flowers in the worship area. Another volunteered to dust the sanctuary. The pastor volunteered to prepare sermons with practical illustrations. They closed each service with everyone holding hands in prayer. They decided to take communion to the homebound.

Worship -- Tap-tap, tap-tap-tap: annoying sounds or vital communication?

Prayer Challenge: What can you do to make your worship more meaningful?

February 24 – Nine Miracles
(Story provided by Allen Cheek)

Acts 3:1-16

I asked church members to tell me stories of how God impacted their lives. I received the following letter from Allen Cheek.

My life started like any other day with a game of pickleball. Suddenly, I felt lethargic with 800-pound arms. I complained of indigestion and said I was going home. Apparently, as I pulled into my neighborhood, I went into full cardiac arrest. Driving unconscious, I miraculously missed hitting children playing on the street. I swerved left knocking down a fire hydrant, then proceeded down the street another five houses before swerving right, mowing down a mailbox before hitting a tree in my neighbor's front yard.

A friend pulled me out of the truck and an off-duty paramedic began CPR while someone dialed 911. The EMT crew had to shock my heart 5 times and took over 20 minutes to get a steady heartbeat. My heart started back then went back into cardiac arrest as they continued medical care. I was told that over 30 neighbors circled the team of 14 first responders kneeling and praying.

My cardiologist inserted a stent the following morning to fully repair my heart. Thankfully, I have no further blockage or any other damage to my heart. Altogether, at least nine separate miracles happened that day.

1. No high-speed accident while driving.
2. No children playing in the street.
3. A concerned friend followed me and pulled me out of the truck.
4. An off-duty paramedic was home and performed CPR.
5. The 14 first responders were resilient and never gave up.
6. The 911 came during shift change. Both shifts arrived on the scene.
7. The paramedic's wife was on the street and raced in to get her husband.
8. 30 neighbors surrounded me, kneeling in prayer, as CPR was performed.
9. My kids were unaware and didn't see anything until afterward.

I recall the instant I came back to life. I shared this with my neighbor, who performed CPR. He said: "Do you remember Lazarus?" I walked away with a renewed spirit of peace and tranquility focusing on God's presence in my life.

This medical incident deepened my faith and heightened my belief in promoting health screenings and learning CPR. My life was saved by God who brought two heroes who saw and did something. This miracle has forever impacted my outlook on life. I'm a walking miracle and give all the glory to Jesus Christ.

Prayer Challenge: Share this story with your family or with a friend.

February 25 – Something

Matthew 16:13-20

I visited two churches in Virginia and two in Georgia. All four contain many families and young adults. At each church, I experienced generous hospitality, stimulating worship and opportunities to be involved. But there was "something" more that had nothing to do with size but everything to do with attitude.

I saw this "something" in action as I drove into the parking lot, The attendants were standing in a circle praying. One saw me, hustled over and walked with me to the entrance, sharing how much his church meant, especially the men's group.

In Atlanta, a couple sitting beside me talked about their Bible study group that strengthened their faith. A woman in the "Welcome" area shared how her life changed through a divorce care group. That group became her family when she needed them. She described her church as "a home for the hurt and hurting."

One worship service featured an interview with a police officer, his family and their small group. At a routine traffic stop, he was shot seven times. Members of their group were at the hospital and their house within minutes. For over a year, they provided meals, child-care, chores and loads of prayer and encouragement.

What is the "something" that vital churches seem to have in abundance? The "something" is a passionate belief that everyone can be transformed by God through their church and can't wait to share that faith with others. In addition, each of these four churches have a carefully designed and repeatedly emphasized process that begins with worship but then leads to various "next steps" such as a Bible study, a small group experience or a mission outreach.

All four churches emphasized continued spiritual growth and being a part of a small group community as an essential part of following Jesus. "Circles are better than rows: Sustained life change happens best in the context of community."

Jesus said: What is the greatest commandment? "Love the Lord your God with all your heart, with all your being and with all your mind." A church should help you love the Lord your God, discover your unique gifts and talents, and use them toward a ministry of serving others and transforming the world.

Do you have questions? Are you a new Christian? Have you been asking: "What's next?" Are you looking to deepen your faith? Do you feel called to be involved in community service and outreach? Are you experiencing difficult times? Thriving churches provide "something" to help you find answers.

Prayer Challenge: How can you strengthen that "Something" in your church?

February 26 – Empty Chairs

1 Peter 3:8-12

Garfield the cat sees Odie at the window looking in. Garfield says, "Poor Odie. Locked outside in the cold. I can't bear to see him like this. I've got to do something." Garfield gets up, looks at Odie in the window and closes the curtain.

There was an unspeakable tragedy at an Elementary School in Uvalde, Texas. The following Sunday, I placed 21 chairs in front representing 19 young children and two gifted schoolteachers. Those empty chairs represented real people no longer in school or church or playing sports or teaching a child ever again.

Like Garfield, it's tempting to close the curtain on controversial issues. Witnessing our faith, standing up for what is right, taking a stand is important. Easy to preach but far more difficult to practice. There are many good reasons: We fear rejection or ridicule. We are unsure of answering tough questions.

1 Peter 3:15 Peter says: "Quietly trust yourself to Christ and if anybody asks why you believe, be ready to tell them in a gentle and respectful way."

When it comes to doing something about violence, churches are often just as divided as everyone. Will restricting guns stop the violence? Probably not. Will background checks? Not by itself. But gun restrictions combined with background checks combined with a more vigilant community? That can make a difference.

A man was brought to the hospital after a propane explosion. His face, hands and upper body were badly burned. He was brought in screaming from the pain. The medical staff moved quickly but what soothed him were the actions of a nurse. As she trimmed away his charred sin and applied bandages, she could have closed the curtain and done her job but instead, she quietly recited Scripture verses about God's care and assurance. That nurse in one brief act did as much for the patient as the strongest of pain killers.

Peter said: "Quietly trust yourself to Christ your Lord and if anybody asks why, be ready to tell them and do it in a gentle and respectful way.," 1. Trust God. 2. Be prepared. 3. Be gentle and respectful.

We are called to respond to 21 empty chairs pleading with us not to close the curtain. Do not let these 21 people die in vain. So, what will you do? What will we do? Trust God. Be prepared. Be gentle.

Prayer Challenge: How should we respond to the acts of violence all around us?

February 27 – Disaster Response

James chapter 2

An earthquake in Morrocco, a hurricane looms on the East coast and Hawaii recovers from a catastrophic fire. Recent worldwide disasters are impacting the lives of millions. The Letter of James reminds us: "What good is faith without action? What good is faith if you ignore someone in need?" (James 2:14)

If we take James seriously, churches and individuals must respond. But how? What should we do? How can we help? Don't do this: Don't jump from your couch and fly to the site unless you have experience or skills needed. Don't give the shirt off your back. Old clothes are seldom needed and often become a problem. Don't believe recovery happens quickly. This will be an ongoing effort for years.

After participating in several disaster relief missions and leading our church through others, here is my top ten list:

1. **Pray strategically,** It will be weeks or months before most people can enter the area. Use that time to seek God's guidance.
2. **Give generously** or set aside funds. These funds can either go to an established charity or set aside for a special project.

3. **Contact local leaders,** to see what's being organized either through your church or other connections.
4. **Research organizations,** to see what's needed and what others are doing? You could join a group experienced in relief and offer assistance.
5. **Assess resources:** what talents and skills can be utilized? You may have people in your group or church who could be a critical part of your team.
6. **Choose something,** whether a project or organization or group that you want to support. Then communicate information about your choice.
7. **Promote creatively** through communication channels including social media to allow people outside your group an opportunity to participate.
8. **Provide updates:** Frequent communication is a vital part of maintaining the enthusiasm of everyone as well as recruiting new volunteers.
9. **Build relationships** with those you are helping. Learn their story and maintain contact so that progress can be reported and celebrated.
10. **Think long-term too.** Short-term provides needed emergency aid while long-term helps with the difficult process of rebuilding.

The church is a faith community sharing the joys and sorrows of life together from the cradle to the grave. We all need one another, and we all need God.

Prayer challenge: How can you put your faith in action and help those in need?

February 28 – "We Are the Church"

Acts 1:1-8

A dictionary defines church as a building for public and especially Christian worship or a body or organization of religious believers. The English "church" is from the Old English word "cirice," derived from West Germanic "kirika," which in turn comes from the Greek "kuriakē," which means "of the Lord." So, the church can have many meanings but mainly the church is "Of the Lord."

If you want to know more about the church look at Jesus, study Jesus' teaching, be a disciple of Jesus. I believe this should be the foundation of every church. Jesus was preparing his disciples then and now for a mission. That mission is called the church. Jesus said in the first chapter of Acts:

"You will be baptized with the Holy Spirit. You will receive power when the Holy Spirit comes upon you. And you will be my witnesses, telling people about me everywhere…" Acts 1:8

In the church: You will be baptized with the Holy Spirit. You will receive power from the Holy Spirit. You will be my witnesses, telling people everywhere.

Richard Avery describes the church in a song: "I am the church! You are the church! We are the church together! All who follow Jesus, all around the world! Yes, we're the church together!"

In the verses we sing: The church is not a building, the church is a people. Many kinds of people. Sometimes the church is marching or bravely burning. And when the people gather, there's singing, praying, laughing and crying.

Trying to follow Christ without the help of the Church is like trying to guide a sailboat across the Atlantic Ocean with no wind or current. You can push against the mast of the boat and make it rock. If you push strenuously, over and over you can create a few waves which make you think you are making progress and you work harder but you are still going nowhere.

Mark Batterson in "Please, Sorry, Thanks" writes that every church should be seeking answers: How do you cultivate intimate relationships? How do you make amends for mistakes or overcome trauma? How do you find true happiness? How do you shift the atmosphere at home or change the culture at work?

You find answers by strengthening your connection with God guided by the church. "I am the church! You are the church! We are the church together! All who follow Jesus, all around the world! Yes, we're the church together!" Amen.

Prayer Challenge: How can you strengthen your connection with God's church?

March

March 1 – The Thermostat War!

1 Corinthians 6:1-8

We had a thermostat problem, and it was getting out of hand. Actually, we had a thermostat war!! Does this sound drastic? Well, let me prove my point. My dictionary defines "war" as *"An armed conflict between two parties."* We definitely had two parties who were armed and dangerous.

One group wants the temperature a "little" cold during the winter and "slightly" hot during the summer to save needed money. If folks are uncomfortable? Tough! Because everything is for the church and savings can be used for ministry.

The other side wants visitors to be comfortable enough to take off their coat without turning into icicles or swelter from heat stroke. Besides, any money saved on fuel is spent again on wear and tear on the system.

Unfortunately, the battles were getting out of hand. Every Sunday the war raged on. The first skirmish began as advance scouts from each party arrived to check the temperature. Then throughout the day: before, after and even during the worship service one person would sneak up on the thermostat and tweak it.

Instantly, someone from the other side would jump up

and readjust the setting. On and on it goes throughout the day. Who wins? The battle rages on.

Funny but frustrating. Disagreements pose a danger of distracting us from our mission of witnessing the love of Christ. Our influence as Christians often centers on our ability to lovingly resolve disagreements, even minor ones.

Can we as Christians disagree yet still love and respect each other? Learning how to resolve a difference of opinion over a thermostat can provide answers toward helping us handle really difficult issues, such as our financial crisis, abortion, homosexuality, divorce, ethics, poverty, materialism, pollution, alcoholism, drug addiction and racism.

The Apostle Paul warns: "When you have something against another Christian, why do you file a lawsuit and ask a secular court to decide the matter. Don't you know that someday we Christians are going to judge the world? And since you are going to judge the world, can't you decide these little things among yourselves? I am saying this to shame you." (1 Cor. 6:1-5)

Jesus never said, "winning is everything." Jesus said: *"Whoever wants to be a leader among you must first be your servant."* Our willingness to listen to different points of view in loving humility says a lot about the God we serve.

Prayer Challenge: How can we better resolve our conflicts and disagreements?

March 2 – Ron

Nehemiah 3

Nehemiah is about leadership amidst conflict as the people of Jerusalem rebuild the city wall. In chapter three the wall is divided into sections and groups are carefully and prayerfully selected to be responsible for the rebuilding. Everyone works together toward a common objective. But not everything is quite that easy or organized.

Leadership and teamwork provide direction and stability even when surrounded by chaos and confusion. Good leadership creates an oasis of calm even when surrounded by a raging storm.

Years ago, I started a leadership group for pastors. The purpose was to give them a place to feel encouraged and share ideas. Ron, one of the pastors who participated wrote: "Before joining the group, I was frustrated and angry. I felt helpless to change anything. I had gotten to the place where I wanted to get a calendar and mark off the Sundays until I could retire."

Ron was an excellent pastor who served his churches well. Yet, as he would admit, something was missing. "In our group, I became immediately aware of my limitations and weaknesses that negatively affected my ministry and my relationship with the church. But, at the same time, I also became aware of my strengths. I discovered the hardest person to lead was myself."

Ron became part of a group providing vital encouragement to each other. This safe environment gave him the freedom and nurturing he needed to think about what a leader for Christ should and could be.

Ron wrote: "I have a long way to go, but I am not quitting on myself or my church. I dream more than ever, and I have a NEW passion for ministry. I don't do things because I am supposed to, but I do things because they are 'Right.' I pray more now than ever, and I listen to others more than ever. One last thing! I don't think about retirement so much anymore."

Nehemiah teaches the importance of working together as a team. Ron reminds us that pastors and leaders of all kinds need encouragement. We too need to dream, feel encouraged and see the works of God all around us.

We are imperfect, flawed and mistake prone. We get angry, jealous and full of needless pride. But we have a God who stands ready to forgive us and restore us. God works miracles through our meager efforts, if we will just trust Him.

Prayer Challenge: Are you part of a group offering encouragement and prayer?

March 3 – "No Pain? No Gain!"

Matthew 16:21-26

Zig Ziglar said: "There is no elevator to the top. You're going to have to take the stairs." In sales, I learned: "If I sit at my desk, there are few problems but there are also few sales, few commissions, little income and eventually? no job! Or as my dear old grandpa used to say: No pain? no gain!

As a pastor, I received ten days of training before moving to my first church. At first, I prayed that I would not be asked to lead a funeral. I experienced only a few deaths in my family, so I had no idea what to do, what to say, how to offer comfort, I wasn't even sure what a funeral service looked like.

But on my first day, a prominent church member died. I led the funeral service on Saturday before my first Sunday. The church was filled with mourners to hear me talk about someone I never met but they dearly loved.

Three days later, another died in an automobile accident and four days after that someone died of a heart attack. Before my first month, I led five funerals and before the end of my first year, I buried eleven people. I never worried about leading funerals again. You would think eleven people dying in a small church dramatically reduced attendance. But attendance actually increased. Why? Family members and friends rediscovered their faith and came back.

Over the years, I learned how obstacles, crisis, and tragedy despite their painful circumstances play a critical role in renewing our faith. My tragic divorce led to starting a divorce recovery ministry. A young man facing terminal illness led his entire family back to God. Families needing Christmas aid led to churches combining resources to help many more.

Jesus didn't say, "Take up your cross and follow me" as a slogan to memorize or because he wanted you to experience pain. "Take up your cross and follow me" is a call to true discipleship. Jesus says, "What do you benefit if you gain the whole world but are yourself lost or destroyed?" (Mat. 16:24,26)

Lee Jampolsky wrote: "Ask yourself what is really important and then have the wisdom and courage to build your life around the answer." Ministry presents a choice: settle for less or take a risk, trust God, pick up a cross and follow. I still like what grandpa said: "No pain? No gain!"

Prayer Challenge: How have obstacles, crisis and tragedy shaped your faith?

March 4 – Snakes and Shepherds

Psalm 23

I discovered a large black snake in our dog pen and reluctantly killed it. Several days later, I was called home by my wife to kill another black snake, this time inside our basement. The next day, while cleaning the basement another snake came slithering down the wall. That afternoon I saw yet another snake crawling down from the ceiling of the same room. I grabbed my shovel, but this time I missed, and the snake escaped back into the ceiling.

I didn't know whether to call an exterminator or put up a "For Sale" sign. That night we slept with the lights on imagining snakes everywhere. We called in a wildlife expert and with his help sealed several entrances and never saw snakes again. But the next few weeks were filled with tension. We were getting little sleep. We were impatient and moody, all because of a few snakes.

We all face snake-like obstacles. The phone call from the doctor's office asking to see you. A distracted driver runs through a stop sign in front of you. The unplanned bill in the mail. The boss who chastises you. The friend who won't speak to you and out comes slithering snakes of unplanned difficulties.

Do you remember this portion of Psalm 23? "You prepare a table before me in the presence of my enemies. You anoint my head with oil." The passage seems to be talking about food but that doesn't make much sense in a Psalm about sheep and shepherds. Then I discovered David could actually be writing about snakes. Did you say snakes? Yes, snakes!

In mountainous regions, a "table" describes a flat section of land within slopes. Before entering a new "table," a shepherd inspects the ground for holes which are potential hiding places for poisonous brown snakes. Then the shepherd "prepares the table" by pouring thick oil in each hole. Next, he "anoints" the sheep's nose and mouth with the same oil making the surface too slippery to bite.

Good shepherds who lovingly care for their sheep do that! In the midst of snakes, God, our loving shepherd, inspects "tables" before us, providing safety but when an occasional snake does appear we are anointed with God's oil of comfort and grace protecting us from the poisonous bite.

Are there snakes slithering down the walls of your life? Have they soured your disposition and challenged your faith? Read Psalm 23 again. Read the words slowly and think about what it means for you to personally receive the Good Shepherd's anointing oil of protection. "Wow! I feel safer already. Do you?

Prayer Challenge: How does God provide comfort when facing life's snakes?

March 5 – Lent

Matthew chapter 6

Lent covers a period of approximately six weeks before Easter Sunday. The purpose is preparation through prayer, penance, repentance, giving and self-denial. During Lent, many Christians commit to fasting or giving up certain luxuries as a form of penitence accompanied by reading the Bible or a devotional. Sounds simple enough but I often come up short. A prayer by Robin Van Cleef describes the difficulties.

> Lord, I sense my need of you; yet -- I am not quite sure how to reach you.
> I heard someone say, *'Read your Bible.'*
> But too often the words are like bullets that ricochet off my brain.
> I heard someone say, *'Pray.'*
> But my prayers, hurled heaven ward, fall back to earth like lifeless stones.
> I heard someone say, *'Meditate.'*
> But my wandering mind was lost in a desert of random thoughts.

"Lord, I sense my need of you," but I struggle. I read the newspaper but put off studying God's Word. I pray and wonder if anyone is listening? Lent reminds us: Don't give up. Keep trying. Van Cleef's prayer continues:

> Lord, speak to me through your Word. Let it penetrate my mind and my heart.
> Lord, speak to me through Prayer, and turn the lifeless stones to bread.
> Lord, speak to me in my Meditation, that I may see, amid life's wilderness:
> The way, the truth and the life.

Spiritual growth seldom happens naturally but requires a conscious investment of time and energy. Lent is a reminder of why that investment is important. We pause to remember the life and death of Jesus and to be transformed by His resurrection.

Deepening your relationship with God requires an investment of time, and persistence but your investment will bear fruit. God will honor you and provide blessings. Jesus will help you make difficult choices. Christ will provide comfort through the Holy Spirit." Lent is God's precious gift for you, ready to open, enjoy and experience. Amen.

Prayer Challenge: What will you do this Lent to deepen your connection with Jesus?

March 6 – The Church: Supporting Each Other

Acts 2:37-47

Years ago, I asked a group of men to attend a meeting where we learned the value of supporting each other. We were challenged to name five close friends other than our spouse, with whom we shared our deepest struggles and joys. Most of us couldn't name five or four or three or two or even one, including me. Oh, I have lots of friends, but not that kind of friend. We needed help.

We formed a men's group and vowed to meet every Sunday morning. We had breakfast, shared Scripture, and devotions but we also laughed and cried and told stories. As we met, we learned to depend upon Christ and each other more.

Is that a good description of what church should and could be? A group of ordinary, mistake-prone, sinners coming together to support and nurture each other through the guidance of God's Holy Spirit. The worship service is part of what it means to be the church but what matters is our response after worship is done.

All the believers devoted themselves to the apostles' teaching, and to fellowship, and to sharing in meals (including the Lord's Supper, and to prayer. Acts 2:42

Part of me wants to stop and say, "Wait a minute. That's too simple, or is it?" The early church dedicated themselves to a simple four-part formula:

- Teaching – Connecting with God through worship & scripture.
- Fellowship – Mutual support in the midst of joy and sorrow.
- Sharing – Sharing food, resources, and time to anyone in need.
- Prayer – Deepening our personal relationship through the Holy Spirit.

This is the foundation for any church expecting miracles: *A deep sense of awe came over them all, and the apostles performed many miraculous signs and wonders.* (Acts 2:43) This is still true today.

Even the best athlete can only go so far on their own. Natural ability, the desire to win and dedication to be the best is not enough. Sooner or later, every athlete needs the aid of a knowledgeable and talented coach. Like athletes we cannot live the Christian life alone. This is the teaching of Acts and the foundation for our church. We need Christ and the church in the same way an athlete needs a coach. There is only so far, we can go on our own. However, with a little help and encouragement, there are no limits: "And day by day the Lord added to their number those who were being saved." (Acts 2:47)

Prayer Challenge: Who are your friends? How can you be more of a friend?

March 7 – Pick Up Your Cross and Fly

Luke 9:18-27

A wild goose is shot down by a hunter. Wounded in one wing, the goose landed safely in a barnyard. The chickens were startled by this sudden visitor from the sky. They began to ask the goose, what is it like to fly? "It's wonderful!" said the Goose. "It's so beautiful to soar in the wild blue yonder! The barn looks only an inch high and all of you look like tiny specks from such a distance."

The chickens were impressed. They asked him to tell more stories. Soon, it became a weekly event for the goose to entertain all the barnyard birds. They even provided a box for him to stand on. But the strangest thing happened. While the birds enjoyed hearing about the glories of flight, they never tried to fly themselves. And the goose, even though his wing healed, continued to talk about flying but never flew again.

I find this parable frightening. It's so easy to talk about being a Christian without acting like one. Easy to say, "Jesus is Lord," without turning our lives over to His direction. Easy to ignore a world in desperate need of our witness. Easy to talk about ministry without doing anything. Talk is easy; flying is not; living out our faith in Christ is not. We must learn to flex new muscles, make painful decisions, take risks and continuously work hard at flapping our wings before we can actually fly.

Jesus said: "If any of you wants to be my follower, you must give up your own way, take up your cross daily, and follow me. If you try to hang on to your life, you will lose it. But if you give up your life for my sake, you will save it." (Luke 9:23-24)

I used to think the cross stood for the pain of being a Christian. "If you really want to follow me, you must endure suffering." Not very exciting; nor completely true. Although pain strikes us all, pain is not exactly what Jesus had in mind. If this were only about pain, we would keep "pain diaries" to see which one suffers the most and "pain winners" would go to heaven. So, what does it mean to shoulder your cross and follow Christ?

Take up your cross is about a commitment to a bigger purpose. Christ accepted suffering because that was his purpose. The cross was his ultimate assignment. A bird's purpose is to fly; but she must be committed to the effort of flapping her wings over and over again. Our decision to shoulder the cross of Christ regardless of the cost is our commitment to "flap our wings" and to keep flapping until we finally fly.

Make no mistake: Flying is the best part. It may be safer to stay in the barnyard but look at what we miss. Imagine the beauty of soaring as we ride the air currents. If we always live carefully, protecting our own self-interests; if we make no effort for anyone but ourselves, we will miss the very best part of life — knowing our God-given mission and having the satisfaction of carrying it out to the best of our ability.

Prayer Challenge: Jesus, help me to take up your cross, to flap my wings and fly.

March 8 – "I Just Wanted Mulch!"

1 John 2

I came to purchase mulch and go home but there was a hole in the bag, so the cashier sent someone to replace it. So, we waited. Then, a shirt was missing a price tag, so the cashier once again sent someone to find the correct price. We waited some more. While we waited the cashier talked… boy did he talk. To pass the time, I started filling out the check and asked: "What is the date?"

"I don't know. I don't care. All I know is it's Friday!" he said with a grin. "Oh yeah," he said with obvious enthusiasm. "I love Fridays… because it's party time and I love to party! I live to party!" Before I could respond, he continued: "I drink and party all night long! Yep! My friends and me love to have a good time."

I thought: "Why is he saying this to me? Should I respond? Should I tell this young man he's making a big mistake? Should I tell him there is another way to enjoy life? Should I talk about God in a crowded department store to a stranger?"

Yet, if I say nothing it looks as if I approve or at least condone his outrageous behavior. But if I say something? How do I say it without sounding judgmental and arrogant? In essence, I was in a fix. There is a Bible verse: "And now dear children, continue to live in fellowship with Christ so that when he returns, you will be full of courage and not shrink back from him in shame." (1 John 2:28)

I needed a dose of Godly courage and wisdom to say something appropriate to this young man and let him know I didn't approve his actions but loved him as a child of God. After a pause, I looked at the young cashier and flashed my biggest smile. "Thank you for telling me about your parties. You just made my day!"

This time, it was his turn to pause. "What do you mean?" he asked.

"I'm a preacher looking for someone who needed prayer and you're the one!"

His mouth opened in astonishment, and he stared at me for a moment before he laughed and said: "You won't believe this but that is what my preacher said!" For the next few moments my new friend talked about his preacher. "My pastor still writes me occasionally and the church sends newsletters."

I left with a bag of mulch and a new perspective on the importance of creatively communicating God's message. What we say and how we say it can mean the difference between healing and hurting. Remember

God's promise: "Continue to live in fellowship with Christ and you will be full of courage." As for me? I have a new friend to pray for. Isn't that what being a follower of God all about?

Prayer Challenge: God gives opportunities to witness our faith every day!

March 9 – Church Stories

Hebrews 13:1-6

A woman found herself in the middle of a divorce. She had all the emotions of betrayal, shame, loneliness, insecurity, and desperation. She had no family in the area. A neighbor invited her to visit a nearby church. She was welcomed so warmly that she returned. The friendship and faith of the people she met combined with the inspiration of the services seemed to be aimed right at her. She said, "I felt the presence of Christ. I have never been so happy. I try every day to show the gift of God's love to all I meet."

One member is a nurse at a hospital. She prays with patients. She says, "the Holy Spirit directs me to offer this precious gift of prayer. Being a patient at a hospital can be an overwhelming experience." She feels called to offer the healing comfort of God.

Following a hurricane, the call went out to assemble flood buckets filled with items that enable people to begin the cleaning up after a flood. Within days, hundreds of buckets were assembled by several churches and shipped to where they were needed.

At youth camp, crews were assembled for work projects. One group took on the job of building a wheelchair ramp for an elderly woman with health conditions. She seldom left her home because of the steps. After the ramp was completed, the woman smiled and told the group her wheelchair bound sister could now visit. When they left, the woman and her sister were in the living room together for the first time in many years.

A letter: "We host dinners for those who need a home-cooked meal. Recently, we placed prayer cards on the tables. The concerns written are shared with our prayer team. Many of our guests reach for the prayer cards soon after finding their seats."

When newspapers were filled with news of violence, a youth director asked the congregation to bake cookies and the youth delivered them to police and fire stations, so we could say, "Thank you and we are praying for you."

These everyday life-changing miracles bear testimony to the critical role of God's church. Some of the most exciting and fulfilling moments of life happen through a church or church member. Attending church should lead to deepening relationships followed by ministry and missions throughout our community and world.

An email: "Thank you for responding so quickly to my prayer request! I felt a sense of hope, and quite literally knew that it was God's love and mercy working through your prayer team. What comfort it brings to know God still works in my life! I don't feel so isolated and alone and am happy to be alive. I know there is a network of spiritually-fit people who truly care and are praying for me!"

Prayer Challenge: How can you be the church for someone today?

March 10 – Evangelism?

Romans 3:21-26

My home church supported a mission ship offering free books, and other supplies to poorer countries. They also sponsored students who volunteered to do evangelism wherever the ship docked. In each city, the ship would open the library and give out books and supplies. The students would go into town passing out tracts and talking about Jesus. People would often talk about their faith and how Christ impacted them.

A few years ago, they visited my city to thank their supporters. They opened the library to give out free books and supplies. The students went into town passing out tracts and talking about Jesus. Can you guess what happened? It's not pretty. They were yelled at, ignored and shoved aside. Their tracts were often thrown into the trash.

We are bombarded with so many messages damaging our trust toward anything religious. Maybe, it's because we saw evangelists pleading for money while traveling in private jets. Or, it's a stranger who shakes your hand and says, "If you died today, do you know where you're going?" Evangelism has gotten a bad rap that in some ways is deserved. Does this mean we should stop all evangelism? Of course not! There is a form of evangelism that is still very effective even today.

What if you knew that by simply saying hello to a neighbor or listening more closely to a friend you could impact that person forever? This has nothing to do with methods and everything to do with taking a genuine interest in someone, allowing God to lead you out of your comfort zone and in your own way, help another person see Jesus in you.

Paul wrote: "But now God has shown us a way to be made right with him without keeping the requirements of the law, as was promised in the writings of Moses and the prophets long ago. We are made right with God by placing our faith in Jesus Christ. And this is true for everyone who believes, no matter who we are." (Romans 3:21-22)

This is a gift God provided for us. We should be excited enough about that gift to share. As a pastor I've learned that I can only personally talk to a few people. But what I can do is enable our church to be a potentially life-changing experience for those who come.

Here are some practical ideas: Take prayer walks in your neighborhood and pray for your neighbors as you pass by. When you ask how others are doing, slow down, listen and ask questions. Be a generous tipper at restaurants and start conversations with those who serve you. Invite neighbors over for coffee and dessert.

Wherever you go, God is giving you the opportunity to make an eternal difference in someone's life. Respond to that God-given opportunity today!

Prayer Challenge: Who needs to hear this? How can you creatively share your story?

March 11 – "One Small Step" and Wineskins

Luke 5:27-39

"One Small Step." brings people with different political views together to record a 50-minute conversation– not about politics, but about who we are as people. It's based on the theory that a meaningful interaction between people with opposing views can help us better understand and respect each other and our viewpoints.

Imagine that! An organization dedicated to encouraging people with different political, cultural, and religious views to get to know each other with the result they would find it more difficult to argue and hate each other quite so much. Sound impossible? Maybe, but this idea also describes what our churches should and could be in a world torn by division and strife.

Then Jesus gave them this illustration: "No one puts new wine into old wineskins. For the new wine would burst the wineskins, spilling the wine and ruining the skins. New wine must be stored in new wineskins." – Luke 5:37-38

Wine was stored in an animal skin bag that ages and expands with the wine. An old wineskin with new wine wouldn't be able to stretch and would burst, creating a mess and you lose everything. Interesting, but what does that mean?

Jesus is calling for a faith like "One Small Step" that emphasizes bringing people together with different views stressing that getting to know each other and respect each other will lead to a world where we don't hate each other quite so much. But welcoming new people means adapting and if you are serious about impacting people you must be serious about accommodating new people.

So, Jesus is asking: Are you going to be satisfied with your own religiosity and spiritual growth or will you be serious about helping others discover and deepen their relationship with God? Then Jesus says, *"But no one who drinks the old wine seems to want the new wine. 'The old is just fine,' they say."* (v39)

Accommodate and listen to new people? Change the way we worship and serve our community? Why? The old ways are fine. They need to change to be more like me and do what I do, say what I say, believe what I believe. And then churches look around in confusion: Hey, where did everybody go?

Jesus is calling for a faith that emphasizes including others. But welcoming new people means adapting and if you are serious about impacting people you must be willing to accommodate them. The world seems more divisive than ever, but I believe we have an opportunity to offer healing. Like "One Small Step" the church has the opportunity to bring people together rather than stay divided.

Prayer Challenge: How well do you welcome new people and new ideas?

March 12 – Perseverance During Tragedy

Isaiah 50:7-10

"I'm going to die!" were the first words of a young man who asked to meet me at church. He had just been told by doctors about a rare form of cancer along with other medical complications that would make it impossible for him to survive more than a year.

What could I say that could possibly ease the suffering this man faced? For a while there was only silence and weeping. But what he said next sent a cold chill down my spine. "I don't know if I can face what is going to happen. Maybe I should end it now!"

Was he serious? Was he just expressing frustration? We could have discussed the whole issue of suicide but this young man did not want to hear a discussion. He wanted honest answers on how to face an extraordinary tragedy with no miracle in sight.

Many of us are left on occasion with broken bodies, broken relationships and broken futures. We pray and nothing changes but in the struggle God asks us to persevere.

Isaiah wrote: "If I walk in darkness without one ray of light--" Is that what this young man felt: Darkness with no light anywhere? Is this a Biblical signal to give up? No! Read the rest of the verse: "If I walk in darkness without one ray of light, let me trust the Lord, let me rely upon God." (Isaiah 50:10) Far from giving up, Isaiah is implying this is the very time to persevere, to place our lives totally in the omnipotent hands of God.

What happened next to that young man demonstrates how God works miracles. He put his affairs in order, took a vacation and spent time with his family. The family pulled together to surround him. The church and community provided gestures of support and love. He came to know God, to really know God as few of us do. A dying man changed, and his courage became a witness for the family and for all of us.

One Sunday, this same young man and seven other members of his family came forward to be baptized. The final months of his life became a testimony of courage and faith. At the Baptism, he spoke about a song "The Dance" by Garth Brooks: *And I, I'm glad I didn't know. The way it all would end. The way it all would go. Our lives are better left to chance. I could have missed the pain. But I'd have had to miss the dance.*

His final weeks of life moved from fear to acceptance and trust. The funeral service ended with everyone bowing their heads and listening to "The Dance." The words burn in my heart, and I cry every time I hear that song. "I could have missed the pain, but I'd have had to miss the dance." But I've learned to trust more in the words of God: "If I walk in darkness without one ray of light, let me trust the Lord, let me rely upon God."

Prayer Challenge: How has God seen you through difficult and stressful times?

March 13 – A Fire Engine Red, Water Pump
(Story by Zig Ziglar)

John 4:1-42

One hot July afternoon on a country road in the middle of nowhere, John and Bill traveled in an old car with a busted air conditioner. They were hot and looking for something, anything to relieve their thirst. On the side of the road, they came upon an old-fashioned, fire-engine red, hand water pump. The car screeched to a halt and they both ran to the pump. John grabbed the handle and began to furiously work it up and down but no water. *"What's wrong with this thing?"*

Lesson 1. Unfortunately, we do not often look for God until we are thirsty.

Meanwhile, Bill was looking around and pulled out a jar full of water. He said: *"I read that a pump like this needs water to prime it."*

"Forget the pump," said John! *"Let's drink the water now and be on our way!"*

Lesson 2. We all too quickly seek to do it our way instead of God's way.

Bill! Said, *"It's not enough to satisfy our thirst. We have to pour it into the pump."*

Lesson 3. The temptation is to settle and miss something so much better.

Bill poured the water into the pump and began to work the handle up and down but nothing happened, so he stopped. *"Don't quit!"* shouted John *"If you stop now, the water will go back down, and we'll have to start over!"*

Lesson 4. Faith often means taking risks and refusing to quit.

Suddenly, cold-clear spring water gushed out of the pump. There was more than enough fresh water to satisfy all their needs. Eagerly Bill cupped the cool wetness in his hands and felt the sweet liquid completely quench his thirst.

Lesson 5. Trust that God will provide far more than we deserve.

John refilled the jar and placed it under the pump. It was the right thing to do. Then the two men, thirst quenched, resumed their journey.

Lesson 7. Share your gift of "living water." It is the right thing to do.

Jesus said, *"Everyone who drinks this water will be thirsty again, but whoever drinks the water I give him will never thirst."* We are promised the cool, life-giving water of God. Once our thirst is satisfied, we offer this living water to others.

Prayer Challenge: How can you better utilize and enjoy God's "living water?"

March 14 – A Widow's Faith & Brian Masinick

Luke 21:1-4

Jesus watched people dropping gifts in the collection box. Then a poor widow came by and dropped in two small coins. "I tell you the truth," Jesus said, "this poor widow has given more than all the rest of them. For they have given a tiny part of their surplus, but she, poor as she is, has given everything she has." (Luke 21:1-4)

When reading this, you tend to think about money. The widow is the perfect giver. Not content to give God her leftovers, she gives it all. Giving generously is important. But Jesus is teaching a far deeper lesson. One gives what she always gives and does what she always does. She might skip an occasional Starbucks or a nicer meal but the sacrifice, the testing of her faith, the commitment is minimal.

What would it mean if she was willing to step away from her cocoon of comfort and safety and give everything? How would that change her? Would she act differently? What if giving everything meant changing the way you act around your friends, your family? What if it meant changing the way you spend your free time or reevaluating your career choice? What if giving everything meant a drastic change in your lifestyle?

Years ago, I was closer to the faith of the widow, making significant commitments that changed my life dramatically. But as time passed, I became more comfortable. I too need to listen to the words of Jesus and reconsider my lifestyle.

Brian Masinick managed and directed my Sowing Seeds Prayer Ministry for years. During that time, he lost his job several times due to industry lay-offs. Brian experienced heartache and tragedy that would severely test anyone's faith. Yet he has answered the prayer requests of thousands of people worldwide with words of encouragement.

For example, Brian wrote: "For every struggle, there are things to learn, people to meet, and ways to encourage. If you look and pray, there are plenty of opportunities out there, and if you are bold enough to seek them, God will not only bless you, He will also take good care of you, and ultimately reward you. I am not done struggling; neither am I done working hard, doing my best, praying for others, and trusting God for everything. May God bless you and provide a bright path for you even when things seem discouraging. Look for what God is doing in your life, and I am positive that He, in His time, will show you something wonderful!"

Brian demonstrates the faith of the widow. Two people make their commitment before God. One gives a tiny part of her surplus and gives everything."

Prayer Challenge: Help me grow toward having more faith like the widow.

March 15 – Chickens and Fear

Psalm 27

Walking home from baseball practice, I took a shortcut through a neighbor's back yard. There was a chicken coop, but I wasn't concerned. "Chickens don't bother anyone." I knew this because at eight years old, I was cocky, fearless, and dumb. The chickens saw me and scattered in every direction. All except for one colorful rooster. He stood his ground as if daring me to enter his territory.

Our paths crossed, I stopped, and we both froze. Suddenly, the rooster flew at my face. There was no time to think about the proper way to fend off a chicken attack, so I placed my baseball bat between the angry bird and me. The rooster hit the bat, dropped back to the ground and stared at me. Now I was afraid.

Once again, the mad rooster flew at my face and again I shoved him back with my baseball bat. The staring contest resumed. For a third time, the rooster flew at my face and again, I pushed him away. He seemed to shrug and walked away.

I cautiously took a few steps, then broke into a mad dash home crying and sobbing. That day, I vowed to God and my mother that I would never walk through backyard chicken coups again.

We all face scary circumstances occasionally. Some, as with my chickens are laughable. Others are very real, whether it's losing a job, a trusted friend, facing sickness or even coping with death. There is fear of the unknown, fear of calamity, fear of people, fear of being misunderstood or rejected or criticized or forgotten or being mistreated. The question is not whether we are afraid? The question is "how will we cope with our fears?"

David had a lot to be fearful about, but he knew where to turn. "The LORD is my light and my salvation- so why should I be afraid? The LORD protects me from danger- so why should I tremble? When evil people come to destroy me, when my enemies and foes attack me, they will stumble and fall. Though a mighty army surrounds me, my heart will know no fear." (Psalm 27:1-3)

Another version says, I am confident which means more than brave or self-reliant. Confident also means 'to trust, to be secure." In other words, the source of David's confidence is not his strength but his trust in God. Whatever your fears, imagined or real, we focus on God.

We have the capacity for great courage to do what is right and make a difference in our community and world. May God prepare and strengthen us to face an uncertain future with courage, dignity, love and hope.

Prayer Challenge: How does God help us face scary circumstances?

March 16 – The English Teacher

Hebrew 10:19-25

My eighth grade English teacher lived and breathed literature and the theater. Once a successful actress she encouraged us to read dramatically. Shakespeare came to life under her tutelage. She occasionally asked me to assist her and advised me to become more involved in drama. So, I began taking classes and even appeared in a few plays.

Because of my interest in literature and drama, I signed up in college for Oral Interpretation of Literature. Today those learned oral Interpretation skills play a major role in reading and interpreting the Bible and shaping my Sunday sermons.

Why am I sharing this? I had a talent but didn't know until a teacher offered encouragement. Teachers play a significant role in our education, but they also influence many aspects of our lives such as ethics, attitude and even our career choice.

We have gifts and talents given by God, but we don't always recognize, appreciate, or utilize those gifts until someone offers encouragement. In Hebrews: *"Without wavering, let us hold tightly to the hope we say we have, for God can be trusted to keep his promise. Think of ways to encourage one another to outbursts of love and good deeds."*

To encourage means to inspire or fill another with courage. We hold on to our hope by trusting God and inspiring others with courage. An English teacher offered encouragement by giving me opportunities to utilize hidden talents. Becoming an encourager is more than speaking in flowery platitudes. To encourage is to inspire another with courage. As an encourager, my role is to inspire others to do far more than they ever imagined. With God's guidance we can all be encouragers.

Our lives are full of buried treasure, God placed within us. We spend time looking for that treasure, digging it up, and putting it into practice. Our next responsibility is to turn around and invest that same energy and talent in the lives of others as a source of encouragement, whether providing resources or providing encouragement needed to help someone pursue their dreams and exercise their talents.

An English teacher inspired me to dig deep and find my hidden talents. God continuously gives you opportunities to dig up the buried treasure within you. Then you can encourage others. Your life will never be the same.

Prayer Challenge: How can you be more of an encourager for others?

March 17 – Blind

Jeremiah 17:5-8

The teacher instructed us to choose a partner. "One of you will be blindfolded and the other will be a guide." Everything went black as I slipped on the blindfold and allowed my partner to nudge me forward and lead me by the hand. A once-familiar classroom was now a maze of desks and chairs to bump into. No longer self-reliant, I was utterly dependent on my guide for directions and safety. But the worst was yet to come.

Leaving the classroom, we staggered down the hall. My other senses provided clues as to where we were. Laughter and talking meant other students were nearby. Ouch! That must be a door. The hard surface under my feet indicated a sidewalk. Automobile sounds fading in and out, suggested we were near a road. "A road, with cars?"

"You are now stepping off the curb and onto the highway," said the teacher. Suddenly, my body lurched out of balance as the ground under my feet dropped eight inches. Imagine eight inches with the power to disrupt everything secure in my life. Knowing exactly where I was never seemed to matter before but now details were crucial.

"Stop and listen," commanded the teacher. I heard the familiar sound of an automobile engine only this time it was getting louder. Alarms in my brain screamed, "Run!" But the sound went safely by, only to be followed by a similar sound from the opposite direction. Again, the voice inside me screamed, "Run!" We removed the blindfolds, rubbed our eyes and found ourselves standing in the middle of a highway.

I never fully grasped the fear and helplessness that accompanies blindness before. Is this what God means by spiritual blindness? At first, you think you can manage as other senses provide clues; but suddenly something shifts in your life, and you are thrown out of balance. Your spiritual eyesight becomes crucial, but it is like you are blindfolded. How can you take next steps if you can't see where to place your feet?

The prophet Jeremiah writes: "Blessed is the one who trusts in the Lord and whose trust is the Lord. For they will be like a tree planted by water, that extends its roots by a stream and will not fear when the heat comes and its leaves will be green and it will not be anxious in a year of drought nor cease to yield fruit." (17:7-8)

Jeremiah provides clues for dealing with spiritual blindness. "Blessed is the one who trusts in the Lord" is about maintaining perspective in the heat of difficulties. "For they will be like a tree that extends its roots" is about faith in something better ahead. "Not be anxious in a year of drought" is about flexibility to adapt to your surroundings.

At times, we struggle with spiritual blindness. Our equilibrium is off. We sense danger. But God will help us remove the blindfold and see with a different perspective.

Prayer Challenge: Help me manage spiritual blindness with trust and faith.

March 18 – Seeking the Lost

Luke chapter 15

The stranger entering the church was young and new to the community, struggling with her faith, and facing serious problems. She tentatively took her place in the back as the service began. There was a time for prayer requests. Hearing the prayers, she felt a sense of peace. Overcome, she prayed so others could hear: "God, thank you for bringing me here. Let me receive your grace. Let me grow in your love and peace." In that prayer the stranger found peace and the church reached out to comfort her.

This story represents the church at its best. Someone is troubled, seeking help, searching for God and finds what she needs within the church. I wish it could always be that way, but it isn't. "I lay in the streets. People pass me by, ignoring my almost invisible presence. I'm kicked out of the shelter at 6:30 am. By 8 am, I am in line for breakfast. I don't look at those putting food on my tray. I can't stand being seen by those eyes. No eyes ever meet mine. No one sees me, but I am here."

Both stories illustrate how we often respond to others in need. A simplistic answer would be to say that most of us either reach out with true compassion or we offer help but with an attitude of judgment. Reality is more complicated.

So, how should we respond to those in need? One reaction would be to ignore them. After all, you didn't cause their problems. A better response would be to pray and hope their situation will improve. You could send a check or volunteer with a group involved in helping others. All appropriate but as disciples of Jesus Christ, we are challenged to "do more" through the love and grace of almighty God.

Steve Trapani shared his own story about helping others: I read about Lady Gaga appearing at a Presidential inauguration to sing the National Anthem. She was worried about going down the steps of the Capitol, so they found a Marine to escort her. While waiting Lady Gaga confessed she was nervous and felt this was the biggest performance of her life. The Marine assured her she would do well but then asked if she would like to pray. Right then and there they prayed for support.

Steve then shared this story: "I decided to stop by the Mattaponi Tribe reservation. We provide food and toys at Christmas. While there, I noticed the food pantry shelves were bare. They gave out all the food and were not expecting more. So, I asked if we could send food more frequently? Just like the Marine helping Lady Gaga, I was in the right place at the right time, listened to God and came up with a way to help people in need."

These stories represent the church at its best. Yes, we are to provide help for the least, the last and the lost but if we truly want to be disciples of Jesus we must find a way to work through our discomfort and truly love our neighbor as Jesus loves us.

Prayer Challenge: How can we better respond as Christians to the needs around us?

March 19 – Christians Are Not Perfect

Psalm 103

I read about an ad: "Reward: Lost dog. Three legs, blind in left eye, right ear missing, tail broken, recently neutered. Answers to the name: 'Lucky.'" That pretty much describes my week. "Lucky." Sigh!

Stephen Pile, wrote, "The Book of Failures." The prologue begins: "Success is overrated." Then he documents the worst failures of all time. Arthur Pedrick patented 162 inventions. None were used. Among his greatest hits: A bicycle with amphibious capability. An arrangement where a car could be driven from the back seat. A golf ball that could be steered in flight. I am not making this up.

So, how do your failures compare? All of us have failed and all of us have at times failed spectacularly but I doubt any of us made "The Book of Failures."

I saw a bumper sticker: Christians are not perfect… just forgiven. That phrase assures me that my primary purpose is to do my best and trust God. God honors effort as much as perfection, attitude as much as results. We all live in the shadow of failure and discouragement at one time or another. What worked in the past seems doomed today. It is so easy to become discouraged.

More than ever, we need encouragement from God. Psalm 103 was written by David during his later years when he could look back on his life. If anyone needed forgiveness it was David. On the other hand, David passionately loved and served God. David's life is a study in contrasts and that is the point.

The Lord is compassionate and merciful, slow to get angry and filled with unfailing love. He will not constantly accuse us, nor remain angry forever. He does not punish us for all our sins; he does not deal harshly with us, as we deserve. For his unfailing love toward those who fear him is as great as the height of the heavens above the earth. (Psalm 103:8-11)

God is compassionate and merciful, slow to anger and filled with unfailing love. He does not accuse or punish. His unfailing love is as high as the heavens. God is tender and compassionate. He knows we are weak. He knows there will be difficult years but all of that will fade like dust or grass or wildflowers, quickly gone. But the love, the awesome love of God remains forever.

As Christians, we are not perfect. But we are absolutely, completely and totally forgiven. What an impressive promise from an awesome God.

Prayer Challenge: Take a few minutes to appreciate being forgiven by God.

March 20 – Jesus

Matthew 5:1-16

I visited several Sunday school classes and asked them to give me one-word descriptions of Jesus. The words came easily: love, goodness, humble, divine, pious, thoughtful, caring, kind, devout, meek, gentle.

Then I asked: "If these one-word descriptions were all they knew about Jesus, what would they think of our Lord and Savior?" There was a long silence. Finally, one youth spoke up and said, "He must be a really nice person."

Yes, Jesus was nice but why would religious leaders of that day be so mad at such a nice man. So mad, they wanted to kill him in the most gruesome way possible. Movies about Jesus don't help because they often portray him as short and thin with long hair, almost like a flower child from the hippie era. Why would anyone get so mad at someone who is so nice?

Jesus was no flower child, and he was much more than a nice person! From the beginning Jesus displayed inner strength and purpose that led many people to love him as their Savior and others to hate him as a blasphemer and rabble rouser. You could love him or hate him, but you could not ignore Jesus Christ.

Jesus reached out to the poor and disadvantaged. But his words for the religious leaders were harsh because of their failure to help the needy. In chapter 23 of Matthew, Jesus called out religious leaders as hypocrites and snakes, not once but several times.

Why was Jesus rejected by the leaders of that day? He demanded they clean up their act and practice what they preached. This man of strength bravely stood up to the most prominent people of the area and told them to change or else. Did they listen? Yes... they got rid of the messenger. They crucified the Son of God.

And then, this man of immense strength, says to people who rejected him, who shouted "crucify him," who watched as he was lashed and beaten, nailed to a cross and left to die. He said: "Forgive them for they know not what they do." When the God who loved us enough to became human and endure a cruel agonizing death on the cross, I listen with respect and devotion.

C.S. Lewis wrote: "A man who said the sort of things Jesus said wouldn't be a great moral teacher. He'd be a lunatic. You must make your choice. Either this man was and is the Son of God, or else a madman or something worse."

Prayer Challenge: Jesus is expecting a response from us. This Lenten season is an opportunity to dig into your Bible and learn what Jesus is saying to you.

March 21 – Clown Communion

Matthew chapter 27

During worship, two clowns entered the sanctuary. Why would two clowns come to a church worship service? The clowns carried a gift box and set it on a table ordinarily used for serving communion. There was a tag on the box that said, "From God to You."

The song playing: "Oh, Lamb of God, sweet Lamb of God. I love the Holy Lamb of God. Oh, wash me in His precious blood. My Jesus Christ the Lamb of God."

They opened the gift box and took out items clapping their hands in excitement. There was a nativity set followed by a cup and plate used for communion. Then they reached in and revealed a loaf of French bread and a white cloth. There was a moment of confusion, then one clown smiled and wrapped the cloth around the bread and gently held it as if it was a newborn baby. She proudly showed her baby to all of us.

The first verse of Lamb of God: "Your only Son no sin to hide. But You have sent Him from Your side. To walk upon this guilty sod and to become the Lamb of God."

The other clown reached in and pulled out a cross, a crown of thorns and a large nail. They looked at each other in confusion. Then a look of horror came over both clowns as they realized what was to happen next. The clown holding the cross sadly motioned for the baby, the loaf of bread. At first, the clown shook her head, "No!" and began to cry. Then slowly and sadly, she handed the child/bread to the other clown.

The second verse: "Your gift of love they crucified. They laughed and scorned Him as he died. The humble King they named a fraud and sacrificed the Lamb of God."

Carefully the clown set the bread on the cross and placed the crown of thorns. Then she picked up the nail, plunging it into the bread, breaking it in half and displayed the broken pieces to the shocked congregation, most of whom were openly crying.

"Oh, Lamb of God, sweet Lamb of God. I love the Holy Lamb of God. Oh, wash me in His precious blood. My Jesus Christ the Lamb of God."

Jesus came to earth with a mission that includes teaching, healing and yes... crucifixion and death. Jesus' cruel death is followed by the miracle of resurrection and the promise of new life. We respond knowing we are a part of that mission as God's church.

Prayer Challenge: How does Jesus death and resurrection impact your life today?

March 22 – "Jesus Christ Superstar"

Luke 19:29-48

Every year about this time I listen to "Jesus Christ Superstar" a popular rock opera during my teenage years. One song describes Palm Sunday starting with the crowd that greets Jesus as he rides into Jerusalem on the back of a donkey.

Hosanna, Heysanna, Sanna, Sanna Ho. Sanna Heysanna Hosanna.

Hey J.C., J.C. you're alright by me... Sanna Ho Sanna Hey Superstar.

The crowd is singing and yelling with enthusiasm: *Christ you know I love you. Did you see I waved? I believe in you and God, so tell me that I'm saved.* An excited crowd, shouting praise would be any preacher's fondest fantasy. "Jesus Christ Superstar" goes on with Jesus' response:

Neither you Simon, nor the fifty thousand, nor the Romans, nor the Jews,
Nor Judas, nor the Twelve, nor the priest, nor the scribes nor doomed Jerusalem itself, understand what power is, understand what glory is, understand at all - to conquer death you only have to die. You only have to die!

The Gospel of Luke says: *"As they came closer to Jerusalem and Jesus saw the city ahead, he began to cry."* (20:41) He cried? Isn't that a strange response for the guest of honor at a parade?

For three years Jesus taught the meaning of God's Son on earth, but no one understood: the disciples, the crowds, the Jews, the religious leaders, none of them. They wanted a great leader; A Messiah who would free the Jews and save Israel. The joy of the crowd on Palm Sunday gave way to concern and finally to anger. Sadly, the same crowds who shouted "Hosanna" on Palm Sunday would in a few short days be shouting: *"Crucify Him! Crucify Him!"*

Before the end of the week, Jesus is arrested, tried, whipped, humiliated, spat upon, cursed, plotted against, crucified, dead and buried. When Jesus was born there was no room for him in the inn. When He died, there was no room for Him in the world. So instead of rejoicing on Palm Sunday for Jesus Christ the "Superstar," we should remember how Jesus responded when he saw the city of Jerusalem: He wept! Maybe we should too.

Jesus Christ Superstar is an excellent musical, but it leaves out a critical part of the story. There is no resurrection in the rock opera. Jesus is crucified, dead and buried. The last song features Judas asking the ultimate question of Jesus: Why? Why show up at this time? At this place? Why indeed? None of the sacrifice makes any sense unless we believe what happens next. Jesus is risen!

Prayer Challenge: Read about Jesus crucifixion in chapters 22-23 of Luke.

March 23 – Easter

John 20

If you walk through a department store and look for Easter, you will find candy; lots and lots of candy. If you read the newspaper ads, Easter is about bunnies and brightly colored eggs. A news article said Easter is about relationships and family. All good things, but nowhere near the real message of Easter.

In the Bible there are several stories about Easter and the resurrection of Jesus. Some report how the women and the disciples discover the empty tomb. They run to discover Jesus is gone. They run back to tell the others but, in the excitement, one of the women, Mary is forgotten. All week she has been a quiet witness to the horror of the arrest, the trial, the whipping, the agonizing hours on the cross and now the final blow – the missing body. More than she can bear, she stands outside the tomb and cries.

"Dear woman, why are you crying?" Jesus asked her. "Who are you looking for?"

She thought he was the gardener. "Sir," she said, "if you have taken him away, tell me where you have put him, and I will go and get him."

Then in a beautiful, touching moment, Jesus quietly says, *"Mary!"* (Parts of John 20)

There is the real meaning of Easter. It is in the revealing and the recognition, the knowledge of knowing that Jesus is alive. The hope, the excitement, everything is restored. Jesus is alive! Easter is about Jesus rising from the grave to offer us eternal grace and hope. Lent is about asking questions: Why? How? When? Where? Who? Easter provides answers: Christ has died. Christ is risen. Christ will come again.

I still like Easter candy and Easter eggs. New clothes are exciting. Receiving colorful flowers is fun. Getting together as a family and strengthening relationships is important.

But on Easter morning, we remember and celebrate: Christ has died. Christ is risen. Christ will come again.

Happy Easter!

Prayer Challenge: Read John 20 and pray Jesus' resurrection and what it means.

March 24 – Now What?

John 3:1-21

As we would say in the south, "I was raised right!" My family attended church off and on. I participated in Christmas programs, sang in a choir and was active in youth groups, but I remember thinking church was boring. In college, I could do what I wanted which did not include attending church. There were a couple of active adult years, but I soon drifted away again. My excuse? "I work six days a week in a suit and tie. Why dress up on my only day off?" I was among the many raised in church, exposed to the teachings of Jesus, but chose to stay away.

But at the same time, there was a growing dissatisfaction with my life and a question that haunted me: "Is this all there is? Now what?" Obviously, something happened that changed me and answered my "Now What?" questions.

Today, people who attend church are in the minority. At least one, maybe two generations have grown up with no church experience.

In the Bible, Jesus talks to Nicodemus, a respected leader. He's the equivalent of a pastor who helps others deepen their relationship with God. Nicodemus approaches Jesus as a fellow professional looking for a mutual sharing of ideas.

Imagine this: I, as a pastor, say to Jesus, *"I know God sent you."* (John 3:2)

Jesus replies, "Unless you are born again, you cannot see the Kingdom of God."

"Excuse me? I already am a follower of God. I teach others how to follow God. I am old and retired. *How can an old man go back to being born again?"*

Good question: It's one thing to tell someone who has never really known God, they must be born again, it's quite another to say that to your preacher.

Jesus' answer? "*No one enters the Kingdom of God without being born of water and the Spirit. Humans can reproduce only human life, but the Holy Spirit gives birth to spiritual life. So don't be surprised when I say, 'You must be born again.'"*

Look at the key words: Human and Spirit. The human in us knows who God is, but Jesus is promising much more. Knowledge of God can only take you so far. Being born again opens us up to following God through the Holy Spirit.

Jesus is not talking about your unchurched friend. He is talking directly to you and me. We must be born again before we can fully understand the awesome gift, God provides and then we begin to answer our, "now what questions?"

Tomorrow: Answering our "Now What?" questions.

March 25 – Now What?
Conclusion

John 3:1-21

How do we move beyond philosophical discussions about God to experiencing God? Jesus is telling Nicodemus, "You move beyond the classroom of human knowledge to intimately knowing Jesus as your Savior. "You and I, must be born again."

"For this is how God loved the world: He gave his one and only Son, so that everyone who believes in him will not perish but have eternal life. God sent his Son into the world not to judge the world, but to save the world through him."

God loves us so much, He sacrificed His Son so that we have a path to follow and a companion to guide us through the twists and turns, bumps and bruises of our lives. As card carrying, church attending followers of Christ, we must first search for answers to our "Now What?" questions, be "Born Again" and then help others do the same.

Question: What can we do to improve our relationship with Jesus? Be Born Again. More questions: What can our church do to provide needed help along the way? Who do we know that needs you to be a witness in their life? How can you creatively reach out to that person and demonstrate God's love?

I, like Nicodemus need to be born again and again as part of my deepening relationship with God. Prayer, Bible study and church participation often provides answers to my "Now What?" questions and leads to fruitful ministry and mission. The following email shows what can happen when we as a church work together to answer our "Now what questions?" and make a difference:

"A few years have passed but I wanted to reach out and tell you so many things have turned around for me since you helped me years ago. I no longer have to go to food banks for groceries, I bought a house, and my sons and I have a wonderful man in our life who is a Christian and loves us dearly. Financially, I am in a better place. God has changed my life and blessed my family more than I could even imagine. Thank you for being an angel from heaven. Your generosity and that from others from your Church saved my life. I pray you are well and are still helping people in need. God bless you."

We all have "Now What?" questions. Together let us be "Born Again" and remove ourselves from what limits us and plant ourselves in the fertile soil of God's amazing opportunities.

Prayer Challenge: Lord, help me find answers to my "Now what?" questions.

March 26 – Easter Faith

Matthew chapter 28

On the Monday following Easter, a restaurant owner must lay-off three employees he can no longer afford. On Monday, a police officer leaves her husband and three children, praying she will safely return that evening. On Monday, a pastor must arrange a funeral for a young man who died of cancer. On Monday, you must face a world full of difficulties, challenges and crisis.

If Easter signifies more than bunnies, colored eggs and new clothes, hard questions must be answered. Jesus' resurrection must be more than an interesting story. Where is God when the world is suffering? How does Easter Sunday help us find hope when facing Monday problems?

The followers of Jesus likely felt the same way as they removed his lifeless body from the cross and laid it in a borrowed tomb? For three years their lives were based on a promise offering meaning and purpose. They were preparing for a "New Kingdom" and Christ would be their King. Now, they were hiding like frightened rabbits. Confused, grief-stricken and deeply troubled, the disciples faced a Monday filled with anguish and despair.

Jesus Christ made a noble sacrifice, but the disciples could not understand the meaning of that sacrifice without seeing what happened next. They needed to experience the rest of the story.

When you read the story, you can feel the excitement. Again, and again we read how they ran, not walked but ran to find out for themselves. Peter and John ran to the now empty tomb. Mary ran to spread the news. A theologian wrote: "Christ turns sunsets into dawn, nights into days. Jesus turns darkness into light."

Today, we face similar frustrations and disappointments. We take comfort in knowing our suffering is not in vain. The restaurant owner must make critical decisions, but the living Christ gives him compassion and wisdom to provide help for his employees. The police officer faces danger, but friends bombard her with encouragement. The pastor reassures the grieving family and suggests creative ways to honor their loved one. You face Monday morning in the secure knowledge that you will never face the world alone!

Celebrating Jesus' resurrection at Easter is a testimony of faith offering guidance and courage for Monday difficulties. Easter is a promise enabling us to cope with disappointment and tragedy. Our difficulties will someday be a distant memory, but Jesus Christ will always be alive and well! Bet your eternal life on it!

Prayer Challenge: Help me overcome Monday difficulties with Easter faith.

Prayer Challenge: Read John 20 and pray Jesus' resurrection and what it means.

March 27 – 1-800-2Heaven
(Happy Birthday Stephen)

Isaiah 55:6-11

Children ask interesting questions. Many years ago, my son, Stephen, walked into the office and asked: *"Dad, why did you become a minister?"*

I thought a moment and answered: *"I received a 'call' from God."*

Not satisfied he said: *"What does that mean? Did God call you on the phone?"*

I paused for dramatic effect, smiled, and said, *"Yes, God called me on the phone."*

He giggled and said: *"What number did God use: 1-800-HEAVEN?"*

I mentally counted out the letters and answered, *"That's close, but it's actually 1-800-2HEAVEN!"* At that, Stephen grinned and left the room while I continued reading.

Minutes later, my mischievous son came back into the room with a twinkle in his eye and a huge smile: *"I called 1-800-2HEAVEN. Do you want to know what happened?"*

Putting down my book, I said: *"I've got to hear this!"*

"I called 1-800-2HEAVEN and a recording said they were closed but please call back between the hours of 8:00 AM and 5:00 PM Monday through Friday."

So, God does answer *"Calls,"* but only Monday through Friday from 8 to 5.

"Does God really 'call' us? Can we "call" on God?" If you search the Bible, you will find the word "call" appears many times. Are you looking for answers to tough questions? *"Seek the Lord while He may be found; call on Him while He is near.* (Isaiah 55:6) Do you wonder if God hears your cry for help? *"I call on you, O God, for you will answer me; give ear to me and hear my prayer."* (Ps 17:6) Do you know if God forgives you? *"But I call to God, and the Lord saves me."* (Ps 55:16) Are you feeling poorly? *"Is any one of you sick? He should call the elders of the church to pray over him."* (James 5:14)

In other words, you don't need to call 1-800-2Heaven. Simply, find your Bible and look where God calls you, wants you and specifically seeks you out. God hears you, loves you, forgives you and will answer you. That is a promise from God.

Recently, I called 1-800-2HEAVEN and heard another recording. This time a sweet, soft voice replied: "Heavenly Mountain Resorts" and then offered to sell tickets for a ski resort which happily promised a "Heavenly" good time. Happy Birthday to my now grown son, Stephen who still asks interesting questions.

Prayer Challenge: God "calls" all of us to something. How has God called you?

March 28 – Be Still?

Psalm 46

As people of faith, we are called upon to pray for ourselves and for others. Prayer is the foundation of our faith and demonstrates our trust that God is in control. But many of us struggle to put good intentions into practice. What does it really mean to pray? How long should I pray? What should we do while we pray? How do you know God is listening?

Years ago, Dan Rather had an interview with Saint Mother Teresa. He asked her, "When you pray, what do you say to God?"

"I don't say anything," Mother Teresa replied. "I listen."

Dan tried another question: "Okay, when God speaks to you, what does he say?"

"He doesn't say anything. He listens." Then she added: "And if you don't understand that, I can't explain it to you."

Often when we talk about prayer and how to pray, we emphasize what you say or how you say it or whether you stand or kneel or sit but one of the most important disciplines involving prayer is the discipline of listening. After all, God knows everything on your heart. He knows all and sees all, so doesn't it make sense that one of the most important things you can do is simply sit at God's feet and listen?

Have you ever been in conversation with someone who does all the talking? Before you can respond or say anything, they yack on; 125 words a minute with gusts up to 500. Sometimes, people are so nervous; they can't stop talking; caught up in the moment.

"STOP!" A counselor once said to a fast talker. Then quietly she added, "Now, take a deep breath. Do it with me. Breathe." Try it. It's amazing how that can calm you down.

Psalm 46 says, "Stop! Take a deep breath." This Scripture helps us to slow down, take a breath and begin to understand, who God is and why we should come ready to listen. "God is our refuge and strength, always ready to help in times of trouble. So, we will not fear when earthquakes come and mountains crumble into the sea." (Psalm 46:1-2)

Any crisis at times seems like the worst of storms. Such extensive damage. Yet the Psalmist says to us: God is there! Then the word "Se' lah," appears as a note off to the side of the Psalm. It's a term cueing the musician to pause, take a breath. Any artist or speaker understands the power of "Se' lah." Se' lah – Pause – Take a deep breath.

Prayer Challenge: Pause. Take a deep breath. Now pray. More on prayer tomorrow.

March 29 – Be Still? Conclusion

Psalm 46

"Be still and know that I am God!" – (Psalm 46:10 If you want to truly honor God. Be still, not to receive secret messages but to know that during silence the Holy Spirit communicates with us. God transforms our heart, and our subsequent decisions are more likely to accomplish God's will.

Rev. Mary Pasternak, a Better Health Specialist, showed how our heart rate is impacted negatively by stress and anxiety and positively by prayer and silence. When a doctor takes your pulse, they may say your heart beats 72 beats per minute. But this is an average. The time between each beat varies, speeding up or slowing down.

Emotions are reflected in heart rhythm patterns. When you feel frustration, anger, impatience, or anxiety, these rhythms become jagged. We don't think as clearly or perform at our best. However, when you experience care, love, appreciation, compassion, courage, honor, dignity, the heart rhythms become more coherent, ordered, and smooth. We feel good, think well, and perform well.

We hooked up a volunteer to a machine to see emotions reflected in heart rhythm patterns in real time. His heart rate pattern was somewhat chaotic as the volunteer sat in front of us. We were then asked to pray for him. What happened next was stunning. As each second passed, his heart rhythm became more and more coherent. The calm and peace that washed over him as he was being collectively prayed for was real. We could measure and see his heart pattern change on the monitor in real time.

As you practice the discipline of silence and solitude, you find yourself growing stronger not weaker, more purposeful not less. You will begin to understand why you exist and what God has in store for you. You should feel less anxiety and more peace.

During times of crisis, there is no better time to trust that God is not only in control but has a plan of action for you. So, look for a quiet place and listen for God. "Se' lah." Pause. Take a deep breath. Now exhale. Breathe. Be still and know that I am God.

Prayer Challenge: Read Psalm 46 again. Be still and listen for several minutes.

March 30 – Going Fishing

John chapter 21

I wanted to be the perfect pastor, Christian, husband and father. I was frankly more car salesman than preacher. I could be arrogant, cocky and difficult to live with. A pastor was someone on a pedestal, and I intended to be worthy of the highest pedestal of all. Until one day, I fell off and hit the ground hard. My first wife, who never wanted me to be a pastor, packed up much of what we owned in a borrowed pick-up and drove away, leaving two crying children and a confused husband.

The next morning, there was a knock on my door. I was greeted by a smiling young couple, there for premarital counseling in preparation for their upcoming wedding. As I walked them through the disaster zone of my living room, this sweet young couple went from smiles to looks of horror. I told them what happened and if they decided to look for another pastor, I would certainly understand. Surprisingly, they stayed with me.

A few days later, there was a phone call from the owner of several businesses and my former boss. He called offering sympathy and then tempted me with a lucrative job offer. I almost said, "Yes!"

Why am I writing this? Because this is how I identify with chapter 21 of John. Peter could be arrogant, cocky, loud, and boisterous. But Peter messed up. He failed Jesus at a critical time by denying him, not once but three times. When Jesus rose from the dead you hear a lot from the disciples, but not Peter. Until a few days later when Peter suddenly says to the disciples, "I'm going fishing!"

Pick up a line, bait a hook, drop a net, and go fishing. That's the answer. Must be safer than being a disciple. After all, look what happened to Jesus! Fishing is an opportunity to get away, to relax, but this kind of fishing is not Peter.

Fishing was Peter's livelihood for years. He wasn't simply going fishing. Peter was quitting. He was a failure as a disciple, so it was time to pack it in. "I'm going fishing. At least, I can still do that. Yeah, I'm going fishing." The other disciples eagerly join him.

So, they go fishing, all night long, throwing the net out, setting it, hauling it in, hour after long tedious hour and they get zip, nada. Peter, the expert fisherman gets, nothing. Can it get any worse? The one thing you thought you could do yields zero. That was certainly me. Maybe I should quit. I was in bad shape. But there is more to this story.

Next: Fishing from the Other Side of the Boat. Meanwhile, read John chapter 21.

March 31 – Going from Fishing to Ministry

John chapter 21

My life was falling apart. I was considering quitting. Peter after failing Jesus was ready to quit being a disciple and go fishing. Yet, after fishing all night, he caught nothing. But at dawn, a mysterious voice calls out, "Have you caught any fish?" After being out all night and catching nothing, Peter was in no mood, but he calmly replied, "No. Nothing."

Then the same voice says: "Throw your net on the other side of the boat." (Pause) Excuse me? Fishing boats were only so wide. Same water, fish swim. What an idiotic thing to say! Yet, Peter listens. He throws the net and, "Voila!" More fish than can be imagined! More fish than can be pulled into the boat! It is a miracle!

"Bring some of the fish," Jesus said. "Now come and have breakfast!" Picture this: a beautiful beach, a roaring fire, and the aroma of freshly cooked fish.

Now comes the lesson. Jesus looks at Peter: "Peter, do you love me more than these?" What does he mean by these? The disciples? The fire? I believe Jesus is pointing at the boats which represent Peter's past. "Do you love me more than your past life?"

Peter replies: "Yes Lord, you know I love you." Three times Peter denied him, so three times Jesus offers forgiveness and restoration. "Feed my sheep. You are not a fisherman anymore." You failed but you are restored. Then to drive the point home Jesus looked at Peter and said, "Follow Me!" Peter would never be the same.

Struggling with my own troubles, I understood what Peter was going through. I realized, if Peter can be forgiven and restored and become a church leader, so could I. God didn't mean for me to quit. However, I needed to learn critical lessons from my mistakes. I needed to climb down from my pastor pedestal and learn to better relate to those I serve. People are not looking for a perfect, untouchable, unapproachable pastor. They need someone who is called by God to serve with humility, despite their flaws.

We all make mistakes, commit sins, and occasionally fall flat on our face in failure. But when we least expect it, God provides a reassuring presence to fish on the other side of the boat. Don't give up. Trust God.

Talent, enthusiasm and skills are important assets but, it's our tragedies and shortcomings that have the greatest potential to be used by God to shape our ministry. We make mistakes, but we are forgiven, and restored.

Prayer Challenge: How does this story help you recover from your own failures?

More from Larry Davies

Don't miss the next book available soon on Amazon.com:

Book 2: Spring
A Daily Dose of Godly Encouragement:
Medicine for Tough Days.

Other Books by Larry Davies

Live the Light:
Five Weeks to a Life that Shines

Breaking the Peanut Butter Habit:
Following God's Recipe for a Better Life

When A Used Car Salsman Becomes A Preacher...
There Must Be A God!

Sowing Seeds of Faith:
In A World Gone Bonkers!

Message Series from Larry on YouTube:
SowingSeedsofFaith.com/Sermons

"Prayer – Care – Share"
"Live the L.I.G.H.T."
"Now What?!"
"It's Not Your Birthday!"
"What Does It Mean to be United Methodist?"
"Luke and Jesus"
"Acts: The Church Begins"

Printed in Great Britain
by Amazon